W9-AFH-455

QUICK & EASY
window treatments

GAIL ABBOTT and CATE BURREN

Photography by Mark Scott

CICO BOOKS

LONDON NEW YORK

Published in 2008 by CICO Books
an imprint of Ryland Peters & Small
519 Broadway, 5th Floor, New York, NY 10012
www.cicobooks.co.uk
First published in 2005 as *So Simple Window Style*

10 9 8 7 6 5 4 3 2 1

Text copyright © Gail Abbott and Cate Burren 2005, 2008
Design and photography copyright © CICO Books 2005, 2008

The authors' moral rights have been asserted. All rights reserved. No
part of this publication may be reproduced, stored in a retrieval
system, or transmitted in any form or by any means, electronic,
mechanical, photocopying, or otherwise, without the prior
permission of the publisher.

A CIP catalog record for this book is available from the Library of
Congress

ISBN-13: 978 1 906094 60 7
ISBN-10: 1 906094 60 8

Printed in China

Project editor: Gillian Haslam
Copy editor: Jane Bolsover
Designer: Roger Daniels
Photographer: Mark Scott
Step-by-step photography: Alicia Clark and Rachel Whiting
Illustrator: Stephen Dew

Contents

Introduction

Interior designers are often asked to help clients change the way their rooms look, to bring life and character to a new house, or to update an old one. One of the best ways to do this is to look carefully at the windows, to work with the architecture of the room, and to pick fabrics and styles that reflect the lifestyle of the people who live in the house. There's nothing quite like changing the window treatments to make an instant difference in any room.

A simple, all-white space can be given any number of different looks depending on the choice of fabric and style of window treatment. Do you want a minimal, contemporary design? If so, make a plain Roman shade for a panel of crisp color. Perhaps you are yearning for a feminine, romantic style? If so, hang long curtains that fall onto the floor and sweep them back into a soft curve with tiebacks. A traditional, classic interior demands formal curtains that are lined and full.

Whatever your favorite style, create it with help from the projects in this book. The pages are packed with ideas you can make for every room in the house, from the bathroom to the living room. If you have never attempted to make shades or curtains before, there's an entire chapter at the back of the book that explains all the basic techniques you need to follow the easy, step-by-step instructions for every project. Some of the simplest ideas often work the best, such as the Tie-top Curtains on page 22 or the Relaxed Roman Shade on page 144. Both are easy to make and perfect for a beginner. There are quick, no-sew ideas too, if you don't want to sew a stitch. Attach a length of fabric to clips on a rod, or wrap a pole with a length of muslin, and you have an instant window solution that only takes moments to create.

Opposite A small, high, recessed window is made into a tempting place to relax with a padded windowseat and upholstered cornice that encloses the space. Rather than curtains, a lined Swedish shade keeps it simple. See pages 148 and 170 for instructions.

Above This beautiful oval window was too special to cover with drapes, so a length of sheer silk has been edged with a pom-pom braid and loosely hung over a pair of wooden holdbacks. See page 126 for instructions.

If you are experienced at sewing your own window treatments, you'll find ideas for more lavish projects that you'll enjoy making. The Upholstered Cornice on page 170 is a satisfying project, and it may be one of your particular favorites. Or you might enjoy the challenge of the Bordered Panels on page 44, a project that requires sewing experience. Whatever your skill or your budget, there's something here for everyone. Have fun deciding on the look that's right for you.

Opposite Tall French doors need a long pair of lined drapes to eliminate drafts in winter. To make both sides of the drapes look equally stylish, they have been lined in a smart red-and-white cotton ticking. See page 30 for instructions.

INSPIRATIONS

Getting started

When interior designers visit new clients for the first time, they often find that homeowners are a little apprehensive to have someone looking around their house. They wonder if a designer will start laying down the law about the latest mirrored furniture, or try to persuade them to buy expensive fabrics in extravagant swags and tails.

Actually, designers are looking for clues about how people live their lives. Are there small children or any pets in the house? If so, design needs to incorporate elements that are easy to clean, such as sturdy curtains made from washable cottons. Do the clients entertain a lot? This might mean that the dining room is used mainly in the evenings, and could handle luscious silk curtains that drape on the floor. Or is the main living room a place that the adults like to keep child-free, with a separate TV room or family room? In this case elegant, comfortable solutions, such as linens and wools, may be appropriate. It's not until designers look around the entire home and talked to the family about how they live in their house, that they start thinking about the decor.

What's your style?

The next stage is to look at the architectural style of the room. Is it a new house with simple lines and large windows, an older home with low ceilings and small windows, or a traditional space with an imposing fireplace, moldings, and elegant floor-to-ceiling windows? The style of the windows is one of the best starting points when it comes to designing a room,

Right Contemporary style—blue-striped Roman shades at sash windows add a contemporary look to a room in an old house. The plainness of the shades accentuates the simplicity of the windows and adds a splash of color to an otherwise all-white scheme.

but there's one more thing to consider: personal style.

If you don't know your own style, look carefully at the items you want to keep and it soon starts to become clear. Take your starting point from the things that are going to stay in the room. Bear in mind the colors in a faded, but much-loved Persian rug, for example, or a classically styled and comfortable sofa, an antique gilt mirror, or a favorite modern painting or print.

These are the issues that will set you off in the right direction, and you can use them when it comes time to choose colors, fabrics, and window ideas for your own home.

Different looks

A cohesive look really gives your rooms a feeling of well-being, a sense that you have effortlessly gathered together all of the elements, without over-designing. It makes you comfortable in your space.

It's helpful to match styles with the architecture, but not essential. You can add clean, modern lines to a traditional house using simple shades, grommet-topped curtains, and textured fabrics. Conversely, you can add character to a plain house with

no particular architectural features with a Swedish-style shade under a soft muslin swag that's draped over a wooden pole, or with a dramatic cornice and floor-length curtains. Look at decorating magazines to get a good idea about various design trends if you're not sure what it is you like. Tear out your favorite pages and use them to inspire you when you are looking for paint colors, fabric ideas, and accessories. Once you have decided, make all your decisions based on your original inspirations, and don't be distracted by impulse buys.

Contemporary

If it's a modern design that you feel will fit in best with your lifestyle and home's architecture, look for simple lines in furniture and window treatments. Go for boxy sofas and solid-colored fabrics that contrast with off-whites. Think about simple clip-top curtains, Roman shades in classic stripes, or grommet-topped panels suspended from a brushed steel pole. Seek out modern, well-designed accessories, such as sleek lamps with metal bases and plain shades, or simple framed black-and-white photographs. Bring in texture, too, perhaps with a nubby natural rug.

Above Country style—a long drape of sprigged florals frames the windows of this country-style dining room. It's a look that could easily take a narrow frill, or even a pom-pom edging, along the leading edge.

Country

Small florals have always been the epitome of the country look, so you can use them plentifully when you choose curtains that are swept back with a traditional tieback. Mix fabrics, too, by using similar prints in different colorways. Mix and match furniture. Collect patterned china and put collections on display. The newest way with country is to lighten it up and simplify. So paint kitchen and dining chairs in off-white and let the windows tell the story.

Traditional

Classic formal fabrics, such as damasks and brocades, are traditional favorites. Furniture is solid and often features elements of eighteenth- and nineteenth-century English and American design. Mix this look with plenty of pale, neutral tones to bring it right up to date, and traditional

or documentary prints on the walls, put soft throws layered on beds and sofas, and accessorize with plenty of welcoming pillows. Above all, let comfort be your watchword.

Romantic

Pick a romantic theme if you love a light and airy look, and go for pale colors that will make a small room look much bigger. The key is to search out pale, painted

Above Traditional style—rose-covered fabric at tall French windows is complemented by matching pillows on the bed in this traditional bedroom. Simple striped wallpaper, combined with lots of fresh white, provides a modern twist on a classic theme.

furniture, chandelier sconces, and lots of reflective surfaces. Painted floorboards work well with this look, too. It's a theme that is feminine and glamorous. Pick pastel colors such as lilac, pink, and blue, and throw in handfuls of beaded trims on

lampshades, pillows, and window treatments for good measure.

Scandinavian

The elements of this look are simple—painted furniture, bare floors, and simple fabrics, such as gingham and sheers, at the window. The main thing to remember is that the look originated in northern Europe, where days are short in winter, so it is important to let in as much light as possible. Choose colors, such as gray, soft blue, and off-white, for a true Nordic look,

Left Romantic style—a plain set of Roman shades, often seen at the windows of a contemporary room, look romantic and feminine when made up in a delicate fabric.

and let curtains gather onto wrought-iron poles with unfussy headings.

Ideas

Once you have decided on the look that is right for your home and your lifestyle, and found a theme that will allow the furniture and things you love to find their rightful place, use the ideas throughout the book to inspire you.

Remember that the choice of fabric and accessories is crucial, but many of the techniques can be interchanged. A classic pinch-pleat heading looks crisp and modern when made up in an ethnic-weave fabric, but it will have a totally different effect if the fabric is a rose chintz design. Changing

Above Scandinavian style—pale gingham drapes hang from a slim pole that coordinates with the wrought-iron light chandelier in a Swedish-style dining room. The bareness of the room is accentuated by the stone floor, but is relieved by the padded chairs.

the fabric, switching from a short curtain to a long one, or even adding a beaded or tasseled trim to a plain shade, will make all the difference in creating your look. Hunt for braids, trims, and edgings—you'll find them an Aladdin's cave of inspiration. Scour flea markets and antique fairs for mellow vintage linen sheets. Made into a pair of unlined curtains, they will look totally unique, and you'll be able to see them at their best as the light filters through the handwoven fabric.

Proportions

Curtains and shades can make the most
of windows if you use them to change the
proportions. A trick-of-the-trade to make
a small window look much wider is to
hang a pair of floor-length curtains on
a wide pole that extends the width of the
window visually. Installing the pole high
on the wall will create the illusion of a
taller window.

A window that is too tall for a small
room can be made to look more in
proportion with the help of a deep valance
or cornice that cuts down the amount of
visible window. You can make a window
seem narrower if you join curtains in the
center and pull them back with tiebacks.
In a room with windows of unequal size
across a wall, use one long rod with
matching curtains to pull the disparate
elements together. It's amazing how much
bigger a room can look by dispensing with
curtains altogether and using simple shades
instead. The amount of wall space doubles
and the light floods indoors.

Practicalities

There's more to choosing a window
treatment than just color and fabric. It's
important to look at all the practical
elements, too. Do you need curtains
for warmth or privacy? Do you have a
wonderful view that you don't want to
obscure, or is there an unattractive aspect
that you'd rather not see? Sometimes a
window is so pretty that it cries out to
be left just as it is. And if privacy is not
sacrificed, sometimes it's better to do just
that. Problem windows can be dealt with
by other means than curtains. Replace plain
glass in a small, round window with etched
glass, or put up glass shelves at a long,
narrow window and display a collection
of pretty glass bottles.

Above left A basic
Roman shade has
been upgraded by
the subtle use of two
different colorways,
and the addition of
a fringed trim gives
the blind an extra
touch of luxury.

Above right A
delicate sprigged
floral shade has been
edged with a light-
catching trim of
delicate beads which
takes it into a class
of its own.

Left A large sash
window is turned
into something really
grand with long, deep
drapes that pool on
the floor. Made much
higher and wider
than the window, the
drapes have added a
real sense of drama.

Radiators

A badly positioned radiator can be a design dilemma if it's placed under a window. It's not practical to use heavy curtains that can be closed or they will stop all the heat entering the room, but leaving them open will mean a lack of privacy at night. You can solve this problem with simple shades and long panels at either side. The radiator itself can be disguised with a cover, and can provide a shelf under the window for displays.

Left These windows were made in the nineteenth century for the owner of a foundry, and the arched windows, made from cast iron, look stunning with their stained glass lights.

Below A small window ledge makes a brilliant place to display a set of blue-glass candlesticks that catch the light as the sun comes round. The window is too small to warrant a curtain, so the owners made the most of their collection of antique-shop finds instead.

Above Build a simple radiator cover with slatted battens for a problem radiator under a window and put up a Swedish-style shade. The curtains are purely for show, and drape gently either side of the window.

17

Light

Sheer curtains at a window will add a translucent filter to the light, giving any room a softer, more romantic look. Avoid heavy draperies, and install uncomplicated sheers and muslins. They don't have to be plain white—pale pastel colors can be layered, one on top of another, to achieve different effects. In an all-white room, a pair of pink sheers will add a rosy glow, or a shiny, sea-green organza will let in cool light on a hot day.

Privacy

One of the main functions of window treatments is to provide privacy, especially at night when lights are switched on and passersby are able to see inside the house. There are lots of ways to achieve privacy without losing light. While some semi-transparent sheers may help, there are other, perhaps better, ways to keep out of the public gaze. Shutters and blinds are good alternatives. Contemporary curtain clips are a great invention, because they allow you to install a café curtain easily and quickly, and can be changed at a moment's notice.

Fabrics

It's always better to use an abundance of budget fabric in preference to making skimpy curtains with an expensive material, but if you fall in love with a beautiful design that seems to be out of your price range, think about using it as a border on a relatively inexpensive pair of panels. Or, make a roll-up shade that only takes the minimum of fabric to cover the window. Simple ginghams and checks are not very expensive, and look wonderful in most rooms. If your budget is very tight, use

Above Unlined curtains allow plenty of light into a room. Not as sheer as pure white muslin, they have the advantage of providing privacy, too.

Left Soften the light with pure white muslin at the windows and any room will look romantic, especially if you underline the feeling with netting over the bed.

Above Mix a less-expensive fabric with one that carries a higher price tag. These plain, lined panels have a strip of floral fabric along the inner edge of the lining that folds back to reveal of glimpse of pattern.

Left A panel of fabric can be installed on the lower half of a window for a café-style curtain in a bedroom. There's no lack of light, but it's perfectly possible to sit at your dressing table in complete anonymity.

low-cost dress fabrics—even colorful lining fabric can look wonderful with the addition of an interesting detail, such as a contrast edge or braided trimming.

If using washable fabrics, make sure that you wash them before cutting because cotton fabrics may shrink dramatically. For heavier-weight fabrics, make sure they are dry cleaned, first, so that they stay in shape.

Luxury fabrics, such as silk, can carry a high price tag, so be aware that real silk can fade and even rot in bright sunlight if left unprotected. A simple trick is to edge a colored silk fabric in white, or off-white silk, where any fading will be minimal.

Always line silk curtains, and if in doubt, use sun-filtering or UV-blocking shades behind them.

Whatever your style or preference, use this book as a resource when it comes to designing for your home. For each project, there is a suggested color and fabric. But you can use the techniques provided to mix and match headings, edgings, and curtain lengths. Play with fabric ideas and be as creative with your windows as you like. Your home will reward you by being a welcoming environment, and one that reflects your lifestyle and all the things you love best.

CURTAINS

Tie-Top Curtains

Nothing could be simpler to sew than these tie-top curtains made in antique French linen. You may be lucky enough to find pairs of matching linen sheets in antique shops, and this is the perfect way to display them. The uneven hand-woven fabric filters the light beautifully and softens the edges of the Roman shade at the window (see page 138 for the shade instructions). These curtains would look just as effective made in any plain linen or cotton fabric.

YOU WILL NEED

- Main decorator fabric, or antique linen sheets—see right for estimating the yardage

- Matching sewing thread

ESTIMATING YARDAGE

- Measure your window to find the finished width and length of the curtains. (See page 186.) Add 4 inches to the length measurement for the lower hems and ⅝ inch for a top seam allowance.

- To achieve the proper fullness, this heading needs fabric that measures one-and-a-half times the width of your window.

- For a top facing, allow for a strip of fabric 4 inches deep by the width of each cut curtain panel.

- Calculate how many ties you will need along the top edges of both curtain panels. (See page 199.) For each tie allow a strip 27½ x 3¾ inches.

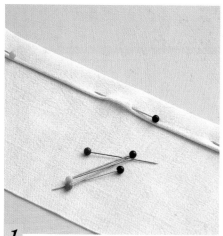

1 Cut out all the required pieces for each curtain panel. Join the fabric lengths, if necessary, to form the finished panel widths. (See page 192.) Press over a ⅝-inch double-fold hem along one long edge and both short edges of the top facing. Pin and machine-stitch in place.

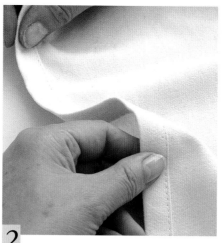

2 Press over a ⅝-inch double-fold hem along both long side edges of the curtain panels. Pin and machine-stitch in place.

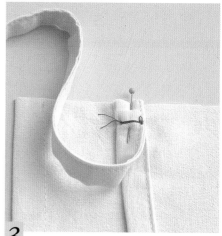

3 Make up the ties. (See page 198.) Cut each resulting tie into two equal lengths. Decide the positions of the ties, spacing them about 6 inches apart. (See page 199.) Lay one curtain panel out, right side up. Pin two ties at every tie position, one tie on top of the other, short raw ends matching. Pin and baste ties in place. Repeat with second panel and remaining ties.

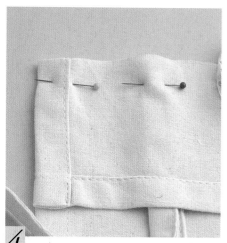

4 With right sides together, raw and hemmed edges even, place the top facings on top of the curtain panels, sandwiching the ties in place. Pin, baste, and machine-stitch the facings in place across the top edge of each curtain panel. Remove the basting stitches.

5 Fold the top facings onto the wrong side of the curtain panels, exposing the ties, and press the seamed top edges flat. Press a 2-inch double-fold hem along the lower edge of each curtain. Pin, baste, and machine-stitch in place.

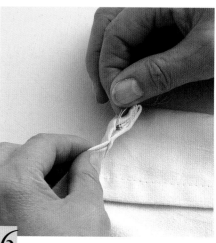

6 Pin the lower edges of the facings to the curtain panels, and slipstitch the open side edges of both the top facings and lower hems together. (See page 190.) To finish the curtain panels, slipstitch the lower edge of the facings in place.

TIP

If you prefer, you can use pretty ribbons for the ties, instead of making your own out of matching fabric.

VARIATION

Use a variety of fabrics to get different looks. A sheer organza, in blues and greens, will filter the light and look soft and gauzy at a window. Use this colorway in a warm room that gets lots of light to add a cooler ambience.

Simple Unlined Curtains

This easy and simple unlined curtain treatment is all you need for a country-style window, and works well with a shade. Choose a timeless cotton gingham or hand-woven linen to make the most of its simplicity.

YOU WILL NEED

- Decorator fabric—see right for estimating the yardage
- Narrow two-cord pleater tape—the width of each finished curtain panel, plus 4 inches
- Matching sewing thread
- Plastic drapery hooks
- Measuring tape or ruler

ESTIMATING YARDAGE

- Measure your window to find the finished length and width of the curtains. (See page 186.) Add 8 inches to the length for the top and bottom hems, and 1½ inches to the width for the side hems.
- For narrow windows like this, one width of fabric should be enough, but you will need to allow two or more widths of fabric for each curtain panel if your window is wider.

1 Cut out the required number of fabric lengths for each curtain panel. Join the cut fabric lengths to form the panel width. (See page 192.) Press a double-fold ⅜-inch hem to the wrong side, along both side edges of each panel. Pin and slipstitch the side hems in place. (See page 190.)

2 Press a 2-inch double-fold hem to the wrong side along the top and bottom edges of the panels. Pin and machine-stitch in place. Cut the tape to fit the width of each panel, plus 4 inches. Pull the cords out to the right side, 2 inches from each end of the tape, and knot the cord ends together at one end only.

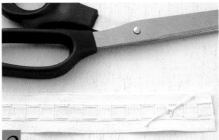

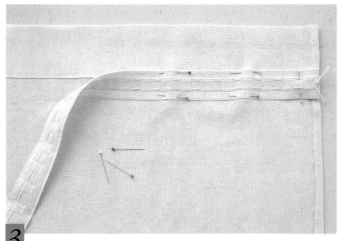

3 Lay the panel out on a large flat surface with the wrong side up. Position the pleater tape over the top hem, lining up the top edge of the tape along the machine-stitch line, and leaving 2 inches extending at both sides. Pin in place.

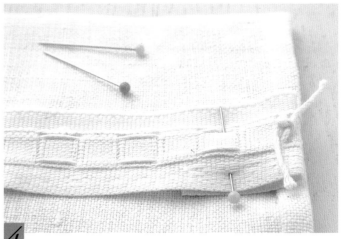

4 Trim away excess tape, leaving ¾ inch to fold under, in line with the edge of the panel, at both ends. Pin in place. Machine-stitch the tape in place, stitching up one short end, along the top edge, and finishing at the base of the opposite short end. Make sure you leave the loose cord ends free on the outside edges of each panel. Machine-stitch the lower edge of the tape in place and remove all the pins.

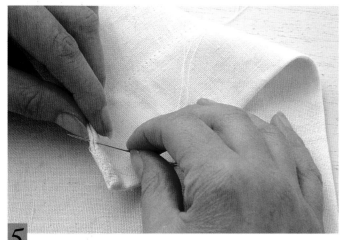

5 Slipstitch the open edges of the lower hem together and press flat. (See page 190.)

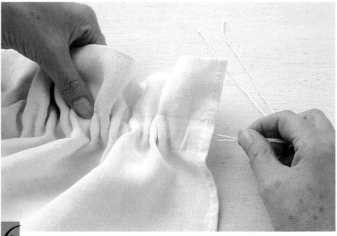

6 Carefully pull up the tape cords evenly, to gather up the panels to half the width of your window. Even out the pleats by hand. Tie the long ends of the cord into a bow and wind into a bundle. Hand-stitch to the back of the tape. Never cut the cords, because the panels need to be flattened out for laundering. Insert the drapery hooks about 4 inches apart, placing a hook near the outer edges so they hang straight. Hang curtains using the hooks from a rod with rings, or a traverse rod.

TIPS

• A pair of simple unlined curtains can look wonderful if made over-long so they are allowed to "puddle" on the floor beneath the window. For this look, add an additional 8 inches to the length measurement for puddling, and cut out the fabric lengths accordingly.

• The instructions for the blue-and-white checked shade featured with these curtains are on pages 126–131.

VARIATION

In many Scandinavian countries, the traditional style is to dress a window very simply, using fabrics like this tiny blue check, shown below. Unlined, the curtains let in the maximum amount of natural light to a well-insulated room, and they are deliberately cut short to allow them to be drawn at night-time without disturbing the pots of geraniums displayed on the window ledge.

Contrast-Lined Panels

Instead of using a conventional curtain lining that is designed to be hidden, line a pair of heavy winter panels with a smart contrast fabric. This will add extra warmth and weight to your curtains, and will make them look great when viewed from the outside too. It is also a subtle way to link the window treatments to other soft furnishings within the room.

YOU WILL NEED

- Main decorator fabric for the outer panel—see right for estimating the yardage

- Contrast decorator fabric for the lining—same yardage as the main fabric

- Matching sewing thread

- Pencil-pleat header tape—the width of each finished curtain panel, plus 4 inches

- Weights for hems. (See page 194.)

- Plastic drapery hooks

- Small piece of calico for covering the weights

- Measuring tape or ruler

- Pins

ESTIMATING YARDAGE

- Measure your window to find the finished width and length of the drapes. (See page 186.) Add 6 inches for the lower hems and ¾ inch for the top hems.

- For wide windows like these you will need to allow two or more widths of fabric for each curtain panel. For narrower windows, one width should be enough.

1 From the main outer and contrast lining fabrics, cut out all the pieces for the curtains. Join the fabric lengths to form the finished panel widths. (See page 192.) Press a double-fold 3-inch hem along the lower edge of both the main outer and the contrast lining fabrics. Pin in place, then slipstitch. (See page 190.)

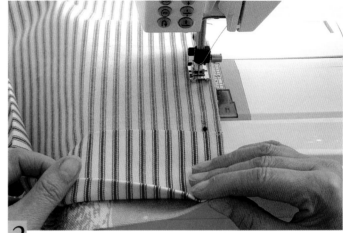

2 With right sides together and raw edges of the outer and lining fabrics even, pin and machine-stitch down both long side edges.

4 Pin the outer fabric and lining together along the top raw edges, then press under a ¾-inch hem to the wrong side. Pin in place. Cut a length of pencil pleat header tape, the width of the panel, plus 4 inches.

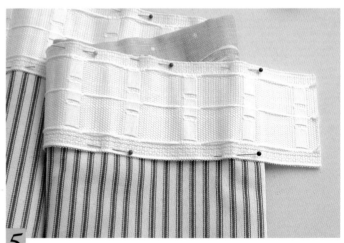

5 With the wrong side of the panel facing up, pin the header tape along the folded top hem edge, leaving 2 inches of tape extending at both sides. Remove pins from the outer edge of the panel, pull the cords out to the right side, 2 inches from the end of the tape, and knot the cord ends together.

3 Turn the curtain right side out, then carefully press the seamed edges flat.

6 Trim away excess tape leaving ¾ inch to fold under, in line with the edge of the panel, and tuck the knotted cords inside. Pin in place.

TIP
Use a simple narrow two-cord pleater tape for pretty country-style curtains, or use pinch-pleater tape to create a more tailored finish.

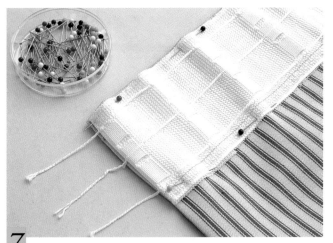

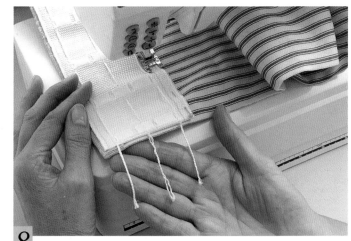

7 Remove the pins from the other end of the tape, and pull the cords out to the right side, 2 inches from the end of the tape. Trim and fold the end of the tape under, as shown in step 6, but leave the cord ends free. (Do not trim the cords.) Pin in place.

8 Machine-stitch the tape in place, stitching along the top edge and down the short end on the inside edge, and finishing at the base of the short end. Make sure to leave the loose cord ends free on the outside edge of the panels. Machine-stitch the lower edge of the tape in place. Remove all the pins.

9 Pull-up the tape cords evenly, gathering the panels to fit half the width of the window. Tie the long ends of the cord into a bow and wind into a bundle. Hand-stitch to the back of the tape. (Never cut the cords as the panels need to be flattened out for laundering.)

10 Cover the required number of weights with calico. (See page 194.) Pin and stitch them into the corners, and at the base of each seam. Slipstitch the hem edges together for 2 inches to conceal the weights. (See page 190.) Insert the drapery hooks into the header tape, about 4 inches apart, placing a hook near the outer edge so they hang straight. Hang the panels using the hooks and a rod with rings.

A single contrast-lined drape, made in exactly the same way as the window drapes in this project, adds a touch of glamour to a feminine bedroom when hung above the bedhead. Make the heading as before, pushing plastic drapery hooks through the tape, but hang the hooks from metal screw eyes screwed into the edge of a half-circular board attached to the wall with angle irons.

Attic Window Curtain

Making curtains for a sloping attic window can be tricky, but here is an easy solution using a curtain pole to tuck a long curtain behind, so it is held snug against the wall. This works well for either floor-length or shorter curtains. Use the same poles and finials for the top of the curtain and below the window. Use an attractive patchwork-style print, which is much quicker than making your own patchwork fabric from scratch.

YOU WILL NEED

- Main decorator fabric—see right for estimating the yardage

- Contrast decorator fabric for the lining—see right for estimating the yardage

- Matching sewing thread

- Measuring tape or ruler

ESTIMATING YARDAGE

- Measure your window to find the finished width and length of the curtain. (See page 186.) Add ⅝ inch to the length measurement for the top hem allowance and an extra 5½ inches for "puddling" at the lower edge (if desired).

- To achieve the proper fullness, this heading needs fabric that measures one-and-a-half times the width of your window.

- Calculate how many ties you will need along the top edge of the curtain panel. (See page 199.) For each tie allow a 3¾ x 27½-inch strip of main fabric.

- The lining should measure the same width and length you calculated for the main fabric.

1 From the main and contrast lining fabrics cut out all the pieces for your curtain panel. Join the fabric lengths if necessary to form the finished panel widths. (See page 192.) Press a ⅝-inch hem onto the wrong side along the top edges of both the main and contrast lining panels.

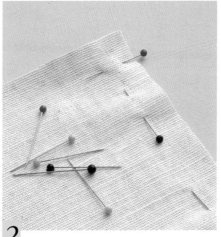

2 With right sides together, top pressed, and raw edges even, pin and machine-stitch the main fabric to the contrast lining, down both long side edges and across the lower edge.

3 Snip across the seam allowances at each lower corner. Turn the curtain panel right side out, and carefully press the seamed edges flat.

5 Work out the positions of the ties, spacing them approximately 6 inches apart. (See page 199.) Open up the top pressed edges of the curtain and, on the main fabric side, mark the tie positions with pins.

6 Pin two ties at every pinned tie position, placing one tie on top of the other, with the short raw ends of the ties matching the raw edge of the hem. Pin and baste all the ties in place. Machine-stitch along the fold line. Remove the basting and fold the top hem to the wrong side, so the ties face up.

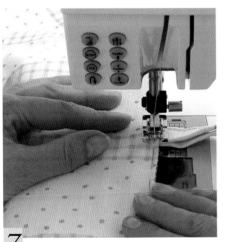

4 Decide the number of ties required—they should be placed about 6 inches apart. Make the ties, cutting each resulting tie into two equal lengths. (See page 198.)

(See page 198.)

VARIATION

In a feminine attic bedroom you can make a simpler version of this clever idea. A single white muslin curtain has been lined and topped with a simple heading tape, before it is hung from a curtain rod over the window and tucked behind a second rod below the window. The result is a pretty window treatment that provides privacy while filtering the light beautifully.

TIP

If you prefer a shorter curtain hanging at a sloping window, first attach the two curtain rods to the wall above and below the window and measure for a short curtain. Turn the lower hem into a casing (allowing extra fabric for this), and thread it on to the lower curtain rod to hold the fabric snugly against the wall.

7 Baste the top pressed edges of the curtain panel together sandwiching the ties between them. Machine-stitch across the top, close to the pressed edges, fastening the ties in place as you stitch. Remove the basting stitches.

Appliquéd-Stripe Curtains

Make the most of a small kitchen window with a pair of pretty curtains made in a printed cotton fabric that have been given an extra dash of style. A stripe cut from another fabric has been appliquéd along the edges and the whole look has been topped off with a small gathered valance (see page 162), edged with a matching stripe.

YOU WILL NEED

- Main decorator fabric—see right for yardage

- Drapery lining—see right for yardage

- Contrast vertical striped decorator fabric —see right for yardage

- Narrow two-cord pleater tape—the width of each finished curtain panel, plus 4 inches

- Matching sewing thread

- Plastic drapery hooks

- Dressmakers' chalk

- Measuring tape or ruler

ESTIMATING YARDAGE

- Measure your window to find the finished width and length of the curtains. (See page 186.) Add 6 inches to the length for the lower hem and 2 inches for the top hem.

- For narrow windows like these you will need to allow one width of fabric for each curtain panel. For wider ones you will have to allow two widths of fabric. Allow also for a 2-inch hem down each side of the panel.

- The lining needs to be the cutting length calculated for your main fabric, less 3 inches; and the width needs to be the finished width of your curtain panels, with no extra allowances.

- For the appliqué stripes, you will need a length of vertical striped fabric the same length as the finished curtain panels, plus 2⅝ inches for the top and lower hems.

1 From the main fabric and lining, cut out the pieces for the curtain panels. Press a 2-inch hem onto the wrong side along both side edges of the main curtain panel. Catchstitch the side hems from the top edge, ending 8 inches from the lower edge. (See page 191.)

2 Press a double-fold 3-inch hem onto the wrong side, along the lower edge of the main curtain panel.

3 Make a neat mitered corner at both bottom corners. (See page 195.) Catchstitch the side and lower hems in place. (See page 191.) Slipstitch the mitered edges together. (See page 190.)

7 Lay the lining fabric wrong side up on a large flat surface. Press over a double-fold 2-inch hem along the lower edge. Machine-stitch the lower hem in place. Press a 1-inch hem down each side edge.

8 With wrong sides together, lay the lining on top of the curtain panel with the top raw edges even and 1 inch of main fabric showing around the side and lower edges. Pin the lining in place along the side and top edges. Hand slipstitch the lining to the main curtain panel down both side edges. (See page 190.)

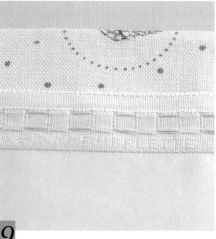

9 Baste the top raw edges together, then press a 2-inch hem to the wrong side and pin in place. Cut a length of pleater tape the width of the curtain plus 4 inches. Attach the pleater tape as shown for Simple Unlined Curtains, steps 2, 3, 4, 5, 7, and 8. (See pages 26–29.)

4 Cut a stripe from the contrast fabric, centering the desired stripe and leaving ⅝ inch along both sides for seam allowances. Press over a ⅝-inch hem along both long edges and one short end. Clip away the hem turnings at the corners, as shown.

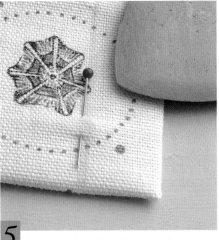

5 On the right side of the curtain panel, measure 1 inch from the center edge, and mark a line from top to bottom with pins. Lightly draw the line using the ruler and dressmakers' chalk.

6 Lay the contrast stripe, wrong side down, on top of the right side of the curtain panel, lining one long edge of the stripe up to the chalked line, and the pressed short end up with the lower edge. Pin, baste, and machine-stitch the stripe in place close to the folded edges. Remove the basting stitches.

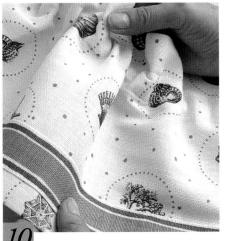

10 Make a gathered valance panel to top the curtains. (See pages 162–165.) Appliqué a horizontal stripe 1 inch up from the lower edge.

VARIATION

You can make a similar striped curtain without cutting the stripe from a contrast fabric. Find a ready-made woven braid and stitch it to a plain fabric in the same way. This idea is quicker to execute, as there's no need to press the hems along the stripe. Simply cut the braid to length and stitch in place.

TIP

If you wish, you can link curtains with other soft furnishings within the room by appliquéing curtains with a strip of fabric used on, say, pillows, slipcovers, or bed linen.

Bordered Panels

Give a long pair of curtain panels a smart contrast trim along the lower and inside edges. The two edgings will look neat and crisp if you join them at the corner with a mitered finish. The matching cornice is featured on page 156.

The matching cornice is featured on page 156.

YOU WILL NEED

- Main decorator fabric—see below for estimating the yardage

- Contrast decorator fabric—see below for estimating the yardage

- Drapery lining—see below for estimating the yardage

- Pencil-pleat header tape—the width of each finished curtain panel, plus 4 inches

- Matching sewing thread

- Dressmakers' chalk

- Measuring tape or ruler

ESTIMATING YARDAGE

- Measure your window to find the finished width and length of the drapes. (See page 186.) Decide on the finished depth of your lower and side contrast trims.

- The main fabric should measure the length of the finished curtain panel minus the depth of the lower contrast trim, plus ⅝ inch for a seam allowance and ¾ inch for a top hem. The width of the finished curtain panel should be three times the width of your window. For a pair of curtains divide this measurement in two. (You may need to join fabric lengths to obtain the correct width.) Then minus the width of the side contrast trim, and add 3 inches for hem and seam allowances.

- The lining should measure the same length as the cut fabric lengths, but the width should be 2⅜ inches narrower than the width calculated for the main fabric.

- Hem contrast strips should be the finished depth of the trim, plus 1¼ inches for seam allowances, by the finished width of the curtain panel, plus 8 inches for mitering the corner. Allow for a backing strip to match.

- The side contrast strip should be the finished depth of the trim, plus 1¼ inches, by the finished length of the curtain, plus 8 inches for mitering the corner. Allow for a backing strip to match.

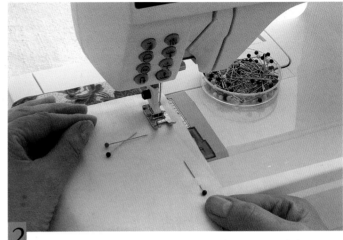

1 From the main, contrast, and lining fabrics, cut out all the pieces. Join the main fabric lengths together to form the finished panels widths. (See page 192.) Repeat for the lining. With right sides together, pin and machine-stitch one long side edge of the lining and main fabric together. With wrong sides together, fold the lining over the top of the main fabric, matching the raw edges at the top, lower edges, and opposite long side edge. Pin raw edges together, then press the folded edge so a strip of main fabric shows down the side of the lining.

2 Machine-stitch the lining to the main fabric around the pinned lower and side edges, ⅜ inch from the edge.

4 Lay the curtain panels, right side up, on a large flat surface. With right sides together, top- and side-raw edges matching, pin and machine-stitch one long folded edge of the side contrast strip to the inner edge of the panel, stitching along the press-line and stopping ⅝ inch from the corner edge. The strip should extend beyond the lower edge. Press the seam toward the contrast strip.

5 Press a ⅝-inch seam allowance to the wrong side at one short end of the lower strip. Open out one of the long pressed edges, and with right sides together, pin this edge to the hem edge of the curtain panel, matching the short pressed end to the finished side edge of the panel, and overlapping the strips at the inside edge corner. Machine-stitch the strip in place, by stitching along the press-line and stopping ⅝ inch from the corner edge. Press the seam toward the contrast strip.

3 Press a ⅝-inch hem onto the wrong side along the long edges of both contrast strips.

6 Lay out the curtain panel, lining side up, with the lower edge nearest you, and the lower contrast strip lying on top of the side strip at the corner. Draw a diagonal line, using dressmakers' chalk, from the stitched inner corner to the outer corner where the strips overlap.

TIPS

• Reinforce the miters before you trim the corners by machine stitching another row of stitching on top of the first, ⅝ inch either side of the corner.

• For a professional look, add weights to the hemline of full-length draperies. (See page 194.) This will help them to hang more elegantly. To do this, hand-stitch them into the contrast base strips before starting step 10.

VARIATION

For an alternative look, when you make a pair of bordered drapes, reverse the plain and patterned fabrics. A striped border against a plain curtain has a very different effect, but you will need to match the stripes perfectly at the corner.

7 Re-fold the contrast strips at the corner so that the side strip lies on top, then draw a diagonal chalk line, as shown in step 6. With right sides together, pin along the two diagonal lines on the contrast strips and machine-stitch together. Trim the seam turnings and press open the seam.

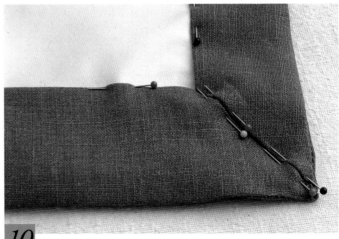

8 With right sides together, and raw edges matching, pin and machine-stitch one long edge of both backing strips to the remaining edges of the attached contrast strips, stitching along the press-lines and stopping ⅝ inch from the mitered corner.

9 Mark the diagonal corners of the miter on the wrong side of the backing strips, as shown in steps 6 and 7. Trim away the excess fabric to leave a ⅝-inch seam allowance along the diagonal edges. Press the seam allowance to the wrong side.

10 Fold the contrast strips onto the wrong side and pin the inner folded edges to the lining along the seam line. Slipstitch the mitered edges and short side edges together, and the inner edges of the contrast backing strips to the lining. (See page 190.) Baste the main fabric and lining together along the top edge, then press a ¾-inch hem to the wrong side. Attach pencil-pleat tape, as shown in steps 5 to 10 of the Contrast-Lined Panels. (See pages 30–35.)

Pinch-Pleat Draperies

The tall windows in this modern room need a dramatic treatment. These floor-to-ceiling lined drapes have been given a professional-looking, hand-made pinch-pleat heading to ensure they fall into tailored pleats.

YOU WILL NEED

- Main decorator fabric—see right for estimating the yardage

- Drapery lining—see right for estimating the yardage

- 4-inch-wide buckram, or stiffener

- Matching sewing thread

- Weights for hem. (See page 194.)

- Pin hooks

- Dressmakers' chalk

- Measuring tape or ruler

ESTIMATING YARDAGE

- Measure your window to determine the finished width and length of the draperies. (See page 186.) Add 6 inches to the length for the lower hem and 2 inches for the top hem.

- To achieve proper fullness, this heading needs fabric that measures two-and-a-half to three times the width of your window.

- The lining should measure the width of the main fabric, minus 4 inches, and the length should be 5 inches shorter than that of the main fabric.

PREPARATION

- Cut out the pieces for your draperies from the main and lining fabrics.

- Join the fabric lengths to form the finished panel widths. (See page 192.)

1 Lay out the main fabric panel wrong side up, on a large flat surface. Press over a double-fold 2¾-inch hem along the lower edge, and a 2-inch hem down the side edges. Catch-stitch the raw side edges in place, starting and finishing 8 inches from the top and lower edges. (See page 191.) Make miters where the hemmed edges meet at the corners. (See page 195.) Stitch covered weights into the lower hem. (See page 194.) Slipstitch the mitered edges together and the lower hem in place. (See page 190.)

2 Press over a 2-inch hem along the top edge and miter each corner. (See page 195.)

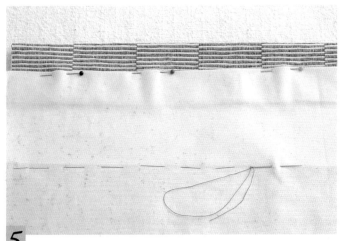

5 Baste across the curtain panel just beneath the lower edge of the buckram to hold it in place. Slipstitch (see page 190) the top mitered edges together and the lining to the main curtain panel along the top and side edges.

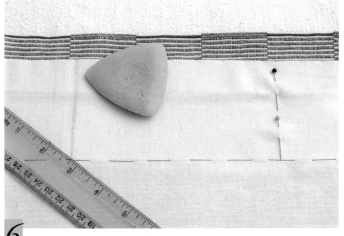

6 Calculate the spaces between the heading pleats, leaving 6 inches between each one. (See page 200.) With pins, mark the position of each pleat along the top edge of the panel. Using the dressmakers' chalk and ruler, draw vertical lines (at a right angle to the top edge) on the wrong side of the curtain panel, working from the pins down to the basted line beneath the buckram heading.

3 Cut a strip of buckram to fit the width of the finished top edge and slip it underneath both the side and top hems. Pin in place.

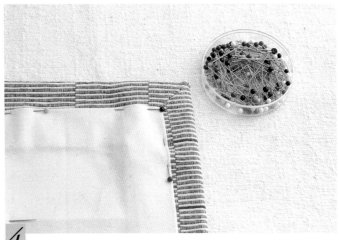

4 Lay the lining, wrong side up, on a large flat surface. Press over a double-fold 2-inch hem along the lower edge, and a 1-inch hem down each side and across the top edge. Slipstitch the lining lower hem in place. (See page 190.) With wrong sides together, lay the lining on top of the curtain panel so that a 1-inch strip of main fabric shows all around the four sides. Pin in place along the side and top edges.

7 With wrong sides facing, bring each pleat together and pin along the chalk lines. Machine-stitch each pleat along the pinned line, ending at the lower edge of the buckram. Make sure the machined line is at a right angle to the top edge.

8 At the top edge of each pleat, pinch the fabric into three equal-size small pleats.

9 Using a needle and matching thread, hand-stitch the top of the pleats together firmly with a few oversewing stitches. (See page 190.)

10 At the base of each pleat, pinch the three smaller pleats together and oversew them together firmly. Remove the basting stitches.

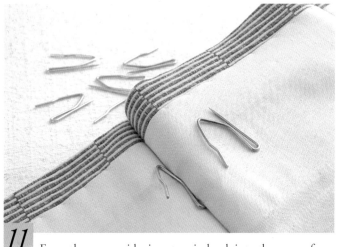

11 From the wrong side, insert a pin hook into the seam of each pleat so that the curtain panels can be hooked onto rings, a track, a pole, or a rod.

TIP

As an alternative to handmade pinch pleats, you can use ready-made pleater tapes, designed to make instant pinch-pleat headings, along with special pleater hooks. These tapes will not give quite as crisp a finish as a handmade heading, but they take the guesswork out of calculating the necessary fabric, and they are easy to sew. Simply pleat the tape to your finished panel width using the pleater hooks. (Hang it from the track if you are not sure.) Then remove the hooks, and cut out the panels using the pleater tape as a guide.

VARIATION

Choose pinch-pleat headings for long, floor-length draperies to balance the pleats at the top. The main project has a contemporary, tailored feel, but this type of heading can be given a blowsy, country look with extra-long panels that "puddle" onto the floor from a simple wooden pole. The amount of fabric needed to make the pleats gives plenty of fullness for a voluminous pair of curtains.

Pinch-Pleated Edged Panels

Show off two coordinating fabrics by edging a pair of floor-length pinch-pleat headed curtains with a contrast fabric. If the main fabric has a large pattern, as shown here, keep the contrast fabric simple by using subtle checks or spots, or by choosing a solid color that is complementary to the main fabric. Alternatively, liven up a plain-colored fabric with a patterned border.

YOU WILL NEED

- Main decorator fabric—see right for estimating the yardage

- Drapery lining—see right for estimating the yardage

- Contrast decorator fabric, for the edging—see right for estimating the yardage

- 4-inch-wide buckram, or stiffener

- Matching sewing thread

- Weights for hem (see page 194)

- Pin hooks

- Dressmakers' chalk

- Measuring tape or ruler

ESTIMATING YARDAGE

- Measure your window to determine the finished width and length of the curtains. (See page 186.) Add 6 inches to the length for the lower hem and 2 inches for the top hem.

- To achieve proper fullness, this heading needs fabric that is two-and-a-half to three times the width of your window.

- The lining should measure the width of the main fabric, minus 2 inches, and the length should be 5 inches shorter than that of the main fabric.

- For the edging strip, allow for two strips of 7-inch wide fabric that are the finished length of your drapes, plus 1 ¼ inches for the top and lower hems.

PREPARATION

- From the main, contrast, and lining fabrics, cut out all the pieces.

- Join the main fabric lengths to form the finished panel widths. (See page 192.) Repeat for the lining fabric.

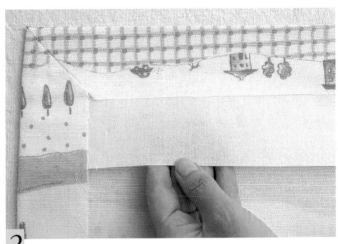

1 Lay the main fabric panel, wrong side up, on a flat surface. Press a double-fold 2¾-inch hem along the lower edge, and a single 2-inch hem down the left edge of the right panel, and the right edge of the left panel. Catchstitch the raw side hem edges in place, starting and finishing 8 inches from top and lower edges. (See page 191.) Make a mitered corner where the hemmed edges meet. (See page 195.) Hand-stitch covered weights into the lower hem. (See page 194.) Slipstitch the mitered edges together and the lower hem in place. (See page 190.)

2 Press a 1-inch hem along the top edge of the main panel. Make a mitered corner where the hemmed edges meet. (See page 195.) Slipstitch the mitered edges together. (See page 190.) Cut a strip of buckram to fit the width of the top edge and slip it underneath the side and top hems. Pin in place.

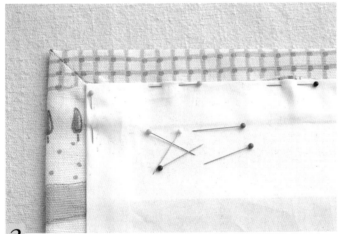

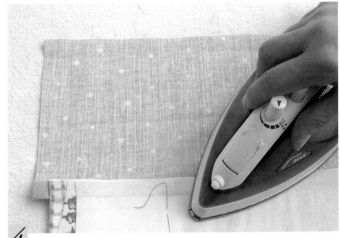

3 Lay the lining out, wrong side up, on a flat surface. Press a double-fold 2-inch hem along the lower edge, and a single 1-inch hem along the top edge, down the right side edge for the right panel and the left side edge for the left panel. Slipstitch the lower hems. (See page 190.) With wrong sides together, lay the lining on top of the curtain panel with raw side edges even, leaving a 1-inch border of main fabric showing along the pressed top, lower, and hemmed side edges. Pin and slipstitch the lining to the curtain panel along the finished top and side edges.

4 Baste across the curtain panel just beneath the lower edge of the buckram to hold it in place. With right sides together, pin and machine-stitch one long edge of each contrast fabric strip to the raw edges of the curtain panels, extending the strip ⅝ inch at the top and lower edges. Press the seams toward the contrast strips.

TIP

The panels shown here have a double pinch-pleat heading, but you can apply this decorative edging technique to curtains with any heading style.

5 Press a single ⅝-inch hem along the top, lower, and long side edges of the contrast strip.

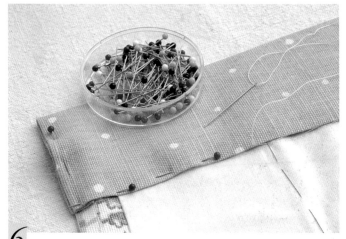

6 Fold the contrast strip to the wrong side, down its length, and pin the long pressed edge to the machine-stitch line of the seam. Slipstitch the strips in place along the long side edges, and across the open top and lower edges, to close. (See page 190.)

7 Calculate the spaces between the heading pleats and machine-stitch together as shown for Pinch-Pleat Draperies, steps 6 and 7. (See pages 52–53.) At the top of each pleat, pinch the fabric into two smaller pleats of equal size.

8 Using a needle and matching thread, hand-stitch the top of the pleats together firmly with a few oversewing stitches. (See page 190.)

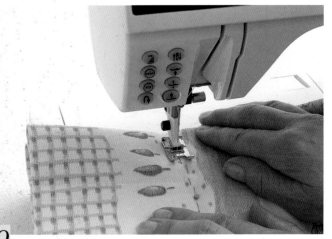

9 Fold each pleat in half vertically and at the base of the buckram, pin, and machine-stitch across the pleats, by stitching through all layers of fabric, from the folded edges to the vertical stitched-line. Remove the basting stitches. From the wrong side, insert a pin hook into the seam of each pleat so that the curtain panels can be hooked onto a track or pole. (See step 11 of Pinch-Pleat Draperies on page 54.)

VARIATIONS

Right: For a dramatic window treatment that combines contemporary design with a more formal look, a pair of edged drapes is hung from a white-painted pole, and stitched together for a depth of a few inches at the top. Long, tasseled tiebacks hold the drapes back from the window. A Roman shade made in a contrasting fabric completes the look.

Left: For a softer look, a pair of creamy bedroom curtains have been edged with a pale blue border, and are left to drape naturally to the floor. Furniture and bed linen echo the theme, but the scheme is livened up with touches of darker blue stripes.

Ruffle-Edged Curtains

Gold-striped organza fabric transforms this tiny attic bedroom window into something glamorous, with panels that swing out from the windows on hinged drapery-arms. This is another good solution where space is limited. Both sides of the fabric will be visible, so choose a fabric accordingly. The narrow, ruffled edges add a pretty, feminine touch.

YOU WILL NEED

- Main decorator fabric—see right for estimating the yardage

- Matching sewing thread

- Dressmaker's chalk

- Measuring tape or ruler

ESTIMATING YARDAGE

- Measure your window to find the finished width and length of the panels. (See page 186.) Add 3 inches to the length measurement for the lower hem and top rod pocket.

- To achieve the proper fullness this heading needs fabric that is one-and-a-half times the width of your window. For a pair of curtains divide this measurement in two.

- Decide on the finished depth of your ruffles. The ruffles need to be twice the finished depth, plus ¾ inch for seam turnings, by twice the length of the finished panels.

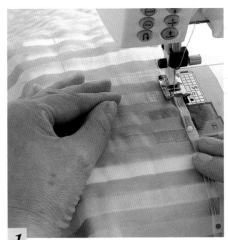

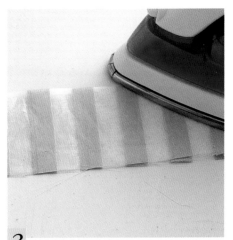

1 Cut out all the required pieces for your curtain panels. Join fabric lengths, if necessary, to form the finished panel widths. (See page 192.) Press a ⅜-inch double-fold hem to the wrong side down one side edge, and along the lower edges of each panel. Pin and machine-stitch the hems in place.

2 Join the ruffle strips together, with ⅜-inch seams, to form the correct lengths of your ruffles. Press open the seams.

3 With right sides together, fold the ruffle strips in half lengthwise. Pin and machine-stitch across both short ends, with a ⅜-inch seam allowance. Turn seamed ends right side out. Carefully push the corners with a pointed object (such as a pair of scissors) to form neat points. Press seamed edges flat, and then with long raw edges even, press the ruffle in half all along its length.

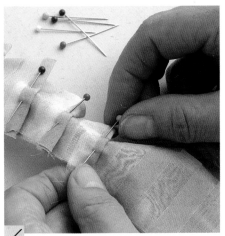

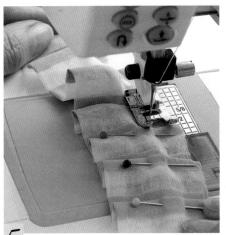

4 Make small pleats at regular intervals along the length of the ruffle strip, until it is 2⅜ inches shorter than the finished length of the curtain panel. Pin the pleats in place as you work.

5 Machine-stitch the pleats in place ⅜ inch from the raw edges.

6 Lay the ruffle on the right side of the panel, positioning its raw edge 1 inch in from the leading edge of the panel, with the neatened bottom edges even, and the top edge 2⅜ inches down from the top raw edge. Pin, then machine-stitch the ruffle in place ⅜ inch from the raw edges of the ruffle, stitching over the previous stitch-line.

TIPS

• A lot of sewing machines have special "ruffler" attachments available that will quickly ruffle a length of fabric—so check your machine manual. These attachments, which simply screw or clip onto your machine, are especially useful for home-decorating projects, because they save a lot of time and effort.

• Making hand-pleated ruffles is quicker and easier if you use a striped fabric, as the stripes can be pleated equally along the length of the ruffle strip. Use the stripes horizontally.

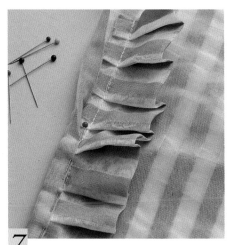

7 Press a ½-inch double-fold hem to the wrong side, down the ruffle edge of the panel, enclosing the raw edges of the ruffle. Pin, then machine-stitch the hems in place, stitching through all layers of fabric.

VARIATION

The ruffled edge works equally well on a pair of long curtains made from printed cotton. Make them with an edge-to-edge lining, but sandwich the ruffle between the lining and the main fabric before you stitch them together. (See page 30.) This edging is particularly suited to a country cottage bedroom, but will look great in any room where you want a traditional look, especially if you make the ruffle with gathers rather than pleats.

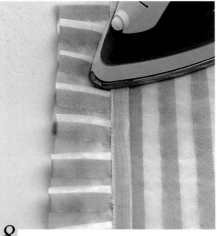

8 Turn the panel over so that the wrong side is on top, and fold the ruffle back so that it extends beyond the panel and the hemmed edge lies flat against the wrong side of the panel. Press in place.

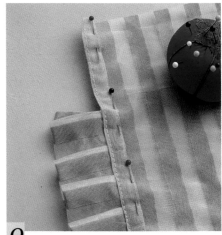

9 Pin and machine-stitch the hem to the panel, making sure you stitch close to the inner edge.

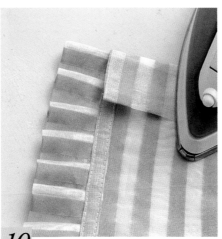

10 Press a ⅝-inch hem onto the wrong side along the top edge of the panel, then press over another 1¾-inch hem to the wrong side.

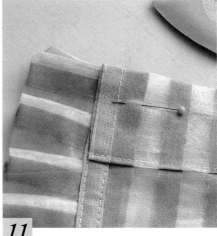

11 Pin and machine-stitch the top hem in place, stitching close to the inner pressed edge, leaving the side edges open. Using dressmakers' chalk and ruler, lightly draw a line to mark the position of the rod pocket, 1 inch above the machine-stitched line. Pin and machine-stitch along the chalk line. Push the drapery arm though the top casing and ruche the fabric.

Instant Curtains

If you are pressed for time, or are a non-sewer, you can still create a pair of beautiful curtains that look stylish and individual. A length of cotton fabric can be simply hemmed at the top and the lower edge using strips of no-sew iron-on hemming web. Then hang the curtains from a rod with rings that have small metal pincer clips. These clips are not very strong, so it is essential to use a lightweight fabric to keep the curtains in the clips. (See pages 132–137 for instructions for making an accompanying Roman shade.)

VARIATION

A no-sew curtain can look very sophisticated with these ready-made clips that simply push through fabric and hold it in place on a slim, steel pole. The clean lines and beautiful design mean these clips would work well in a contemporary apartment.

Two-Tone Panel

Keep out cold winter drafts with a fully lined curtain panel for a glass-panel door. A wide band of contrast fabric stitched to the base of the curtain prevents the single panel from looking too long and narrow. This contrast band also adds an extra boost of color and can link to color schemes used in rooms leading off the hallway.

YOU WILL NEED

- 54-inch-wide main decorator fabric—see right for estimating the yardage

- 54-inch-wide contrast decorator fabric—see right for estimating the yardage

- 54-inch-wide drapery lining—see right for estimating the yardage

- 4-inch-wide buckram, or stiffener, to fit the width of the panel

- Matching sewing thread

- Weights for the hem. (See page 194.)

- Pin hooks

ESTIMATING YARDAGE

- Measure your door to determine the finished length of your panel. (See page 186.)

- Decide on the finished depth of your contrast fabric band, and take this measurement away from the finished length.

- For the main fabric, allow one width of fabric, by the length calculated (minus the contrast band), and add $1\frac{3}{8}$ inches for the top hem and seam allowance.

- For the contrast fabric, allow one width of fabric that is the depth of the contrast band, plus $6\frac{5}{8}$ inches for the lower hem and seam allowance.

- For the lining, allow one width of lining that is 4 inches narrower than the main and contrast fabrics, by the total finished length measurement, plus $3\frac{3}{4}$ inches for hems.

1 From the main, contrast, and lining fabrics, cut out the pieces for your panel. With right sides together, and raw edges even, lay one long edge of the contrast band on top of one short edge of the main panel. Pin and machine-stitch the pieces together with a ⅝-inch seam allowance. Press open the seam.

2 Press a 2-inch hem onto the wrong side, down both side edges of the joined panel, and pin in place. Catchstitch the side hems in place, starting 5 inches from the top edge, and finishing 8 inches from the lower edge. (See page 191.)

5 Press a ¾-inch hem along the top edge of the main curtain panel, and open out the top part of side hems.

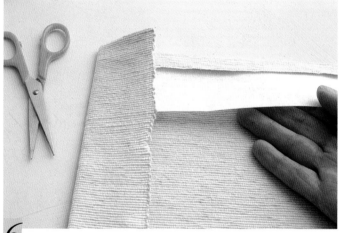

6 Cut a strip of buckram to fit the width of the finished top edge, and trim it down to half its width (2 inches wide). Slip it under both the top and the side hems. Catchstitch the remaining open part of the side hems. (See page 191.)

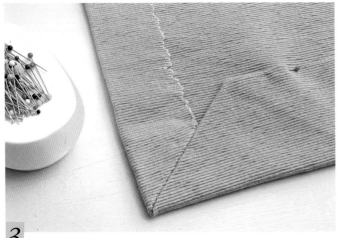

3 Press a double-fold 3-inch hem to the wrong side, along the lower edge of the panel. Make a miter at both corners of the lower hem. (See page 195.) Then catchstitch a covered weight into both hem corners. (See page 194.) Catchstitch the remaining open, lower part of the side hems and lower hem in place. Slipstitch the edges of the mitered corners together. (See page 190.)

4 Press a double-fold 2-inch hem to the wrong side, along the lower edge of the lining. Machine-stitch the lower hem in place. Press a 1-inch hem down each side of the lining and a ¾-inch hem along the top edge.

7 With wrong sides facing, lay the lining on top of the main panel with the top pressed edges even and 1 inch of main and contrast fabric showing around the side and lower edges. Pin the lining in place along the side and top edges. Hand slipstitch the lining to the main panel along both side edges. (See page 190.)

8 Baste across the curtain panel just beneath the lower edge of the buckram to hold it in place.

TIP

If you would like to create this two-tone effect on regular pleated drapes, use the instructions for "Estimating yardage," but remember to check the individual projects for working out correct fabric fullness (width) for the style. Join the main and contrast fabrics together, as shown in step 1, then turn to the individual projects to complete the panels. See "Contrast-Lined Panels" on page 30, or "Pinch-Pleat Draperies" on page 50.

VARIATION

A deep hem in a contrast fabric can make a dramatic design statement if you choose strong tones and luxurious silk. These generous floor-to-ceiling curtains form the focal point of this traditional dining room, and cover the entire wall when closed. The valance is a fringed length of fabric that is simply draped over a second pole fixed in front of the curtains, echoing the color of the hem.

9 Machine-stitch the buckram in place by stitching close to the top edge and again along the basted line, beneath the buckram. Remove the basting stitches.

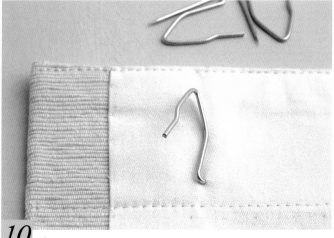

10 Count the number of rings on your curtain rod. Take the same number of pin hooks and insert them into the wrong side of the buckram heading. Place the first and last hook 1–2 inches from each side, and space the remaining hooks evenly between.

Café Curtains

Bring a little privacy to a room without losing any light with scallop-topped café curtains that cover the lower half of a small window. The curtains are unlined, but have a shaped facing at the top and tiny buttons for a decorative effect. The style is perfect for kitchens and baths.

YOU WILL NEED

- Main decorator fabric—see right for estimating the yardage

- Matching sewing thread

- Paper for making a template

- Dressmakers' chalk

- Small buttons

ESTIMATING YARDAGE

- Measure your window from the required height to the sill to find the finished length of the curtains. Add 2 inches to the length for a lower hem and top seam allowance.

- To achieve proper fullness, this curtain needs fabric that measures one-and-a-quarter to one-and-a-half the width of your window.

- The top facing is a strip that is 9 inches deep by the width calculated for the curtain.

TIP

Extend the facing fabric to the hem edge if you want a curtain that looks finished on both sides, but leave the lower hems loose.

1 Cut out the curtain panel and facing to the correct width and length, joining any fabric widths if necessary, with flat fell seams. (See page 193.) Make a paper template for the scalloped edge, as shown on page 201. Press a ¼-inch double-fold hem onto the wrong side along one long edge of the facing. Pin and machine-stitch in place.

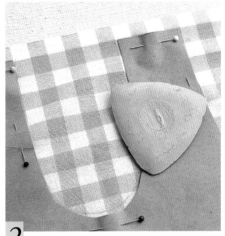

2 With right sides together, place the facing on top of the main panel with the top raw edges level. Position the paper template ⅜ inch from the side and top edges, and pin in place. Using the dressmakers' chalk, trace the scallop shapes along the top edge and down the sides. Remove the template.

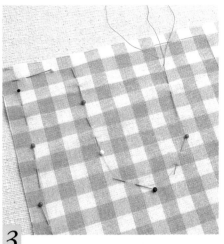

3 Pin and then baste the fabric pieces together around the chalked scalloped lines and down the side edges to the lower edge of the facing.

7 Press a ¼-inch double-fold hem onto the wrong side down the remaining raw side edges. Pin and machine-stitch the hems in place.

8 Press a ¾-inch double-fold hem to the wrong side along the bottom edge of the curtain. Pin and hand catch-stitch the hem in place. (See page 191.)

9 Fold down 1½ inches of the top sections of each scallop onto the wrong side, pin in place, then hand catch-stitch the newly formed loops in place. (See page 191.)

4 Machine-stitch along the chalked lines, then remove the basting stitches. Cut out the scalloped shapes, leaving a ⅜-inch seam allowance around the edges.

5 Clip notches into the curved seam allowances at the base of each scallop, no closer to the stitching line than ⅛ inch. Clip the corners of the seam allowances at the top of each of the scallops.

6 Turn the top scalloped edge to the right side, gently easing out the corners with the point of a pair of scissors. Press the seamed edges flat.

10 On the right side of the curtain, sew a button at the base of each loop, about 2 inches down from the top folded edges.

VARIATION

Make an instant curtain to hang halfway down a window by using vintage lace cloth picked up at a thrift store or flea market. Here an antique tray cloth with a filet crochet border has been threaded onto a curtain wire, letting the top edge of the border drape over at the front. It makes a wonderful screen on a window at street level, and looks delightful from both sides.

Grommet-Top Panels

Falling into simple folds, these panels with grommet headings are an up-to-date way to dress a window. They look uncluttered and sleek with doors leading into the garden from a country kitchen.

YOU WILL NEED

- Main decorator fabric—see right for estimating the yardage

- Drapery lining—see right for estimating the yardage

- Grommet tape—see right for estimating the yardage

- Matching sewing thread

- Weights for hems. (See page 194.)

- Measuring tape or ruler

ESTIMATING YARDAGE

- Measure your window to determine the finished width and length of the curtain panels. Add 6¾ inches for top and lower hems.

- To achieve the proper fullness, this heading needs fabric that measures about one-and-a-half to two times the width of your window, but this is dependent on the length of your grommet tape—see estimating the grommet tape, below. Allow for enough main fabric to fit the length and the width calculated, plus 4 inches for side hems.

- Allow enough grommet tape to fit your estimated panel width, but make sure you end up with an equal number of grommets, and that the outer edge of the first and last grommets sit about 1½ inches from the finished edges of the curtain panel. Allow an extra ¾-inch of tape at each end for neatening. Adjust your curtain panel width to fit the tape length.

- The lining should measure the width calculated for the main fabric, minus 4 inches by the length calculated, minus 3 inches.

1 From the main and lining fabrics, cut out the required number of fabric lengths. Join the widths if necessary to form the finished panel widths. (See page 192.) Press a 2-inch hem to the wrong side down both side edges of the main fabric panel. Catchstitch the hems, starting and finishing 8 inches from top and lower edges. (See page 191.)

2 Press a double-fold 3-inch hem to the wrong side along the lower edge of the main panel.

3 Make a neat miter at both corners of the lower hem. (See page 195.) Then catchstitch a covered weight into both hem corners, and at the lower edge of any panel seams. (See page 194.) Catchstitch the remaining open side hem and the lower hem in place. Slipstitch the edges of the mitered corner together. (See page 190.)

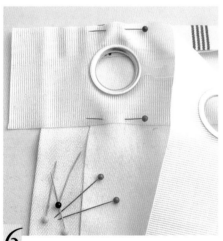

6 Press the top edge of the panel ¾ inch onto the wrong side. Lay the panel on a flat surface, wrong side up. Cut the grommet tape to size and position it along the pressed top edge, ensuring the grommets are facing the correct way for the back of the panel, and that the tape extends ¾ inch at each end. Pin in place, folding under the ends to neaten.

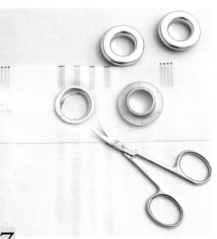

7 Machine-stitch the tape in place, stitching up one short end, along the top edge, and finishing at the base of the opposite short end. Machine-stitch the lower edge of the tape in place, and remove the pins. Using sharp embroidery scissors, carefully cut away the fabric inside the grommets. Don't worry about fraying because the front rings will close up all raw edges.

8 Turn the panel right side up, and snap on the front grommet rings, over each cut-away circle. Press down firmly on the rings, to make sure they are properly fixed in place. Thread the grommets onto the drapery rod, by passing the rod through from the front of the panel first, and finish by passing the rod from the back of the panel to the front.

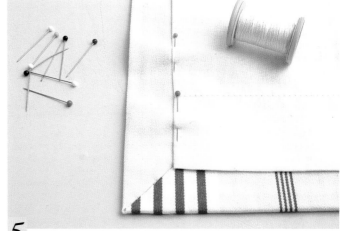

4 Lay the lining fabric, wrong side up, on a large flat surface with the lower edge nearest you. Press a double-fold 2-inch hem to the wrong side, along the lower edge. Pin and machine-stitch the hem in place. Press down a 1-inch hem along each side edge of the lining panel.

5 With wrong sides facing, place the lining on top of the hemmed curtain panel, with top raw edges even, and with 1 inch of main fabric showing around the lower and side edges. Pin the lining to the main panel along the top and side edges. Slipstitch the pressed side edges. (See page 190.)

TIP

If you cannot find grommet tape at a fabric store or online, use large, individual grommets, fixed in place with a grommet punch, a tool that is available in craft stores. To work out how many grommets you will need, follow the instructions for the tape in "Estimating yardage," spacing the grommet centers roughly 5½ inches apart. You will also need to add a strip of lightweight buckram to the top edge, to support the grommets. Cut out the panel, adding 2 inches for the top hem. Make up the panel to step 3, then turn to "Pinch-Pleat Draperies," following steps 2, 3, 4, and 5 on pages 52–53, to insert the buckram, and complete the panel.

VARIATION

The striped kitchen panels in the main project have a deliberately unsophisticated look that works brilliantly in a simple country kitchen. However, grommet headings can look classic too. Choose a beautiful fabric and you'll notice how the folds of the curtain, rather than being full and gathered, display the pattern to best advantage.

Shirred Rod-Pocket Curtains

A straight stitch is all it takes to create shirred rod-pocket curtains. Leave a few inches of fabric at the top for a fancy header that adds a formal look to the design. Edged with a ready-made pom-pom trim, the design is a pretty way to frame a small bedroom window, especially with wooden holdbacks to keep curtains open at the window. Attach the holdbacks high on the wall, to allow the curtains to drape elegantly.

YOU WILL NEED

- Main decorator fabric—see right for yardage

- Matching sewing thread

- Weights for hems. (See page 194.)

- Small piece of muslin for covering the weights

- Ready-made pom-pom trim—see right for yardage

ESTIMATING YARDAGE

- Measure your window to find the finished width and length of the curtains. (See page 186.) Add 4 inches for the lower hem and 10 inches for the shirred top.

- To achieve the proper fullness, this heading needs fabric that measures twice the width of your window.

- For the pom-pom trim, allow the measured finished length, plus 4 inches for each curtain panel.

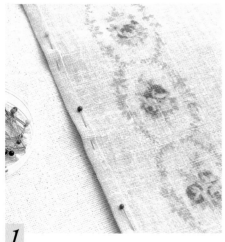

1 Cut out the required number of fabric lengths for each curtain panel. Join the fabric widths, if necessary, with flat fell seams, to form the correct finished curtain widths. (See page 193.) Press a ⅝-inch double-fold hem onto the wrong side, along both side edges. Pin the hems in place, then slipstitch them by hand. (See page 190.)

2 Press a 2-inch double-fold hem onto the wrong side, along the lower edge of the curtain.

3 Cover the required number of weights with muslin. (See page 194.) Unfold the pressed lower hem and pin, then stitch them to the underside of the first fold, one at each side edge and one at the lower edge of any joining seams.

5 Press a ⅜-inch hem onto the wrong side along the top edge of the curtain panel, then press another 6 inches onto the wrong side. Pin in place.

6 Unpin and unfold the top hem along the inner edge for about 6 inches. Pin the pom-pom trim onto the wrong side of the inner edge, along the slipstitched side hem, ending at the top pressed edge, as shown. Slipstitch the tape of the pom-pom trim to the side hem.

7 Fold the top hem back down at the leading edge and pin it in place. Slipstitch the open side edges of the top hem together to within 2½ inches of the lower pressed edge, sandwiching the pom-pom trim in-between.

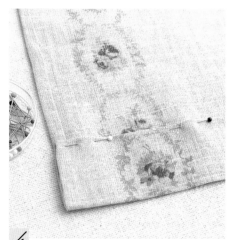

4 Fold back the lower hem and pin it in place, enclosing the weights. Slipstitch the open side edges of the hem together, then slipstitch the top pressed edge in place. (See page 190.)

8 Machine-stitch the lower pressed edge of the top hem in place, then measure 2½ inches up from this edge and mark the position with a row of pins. Machine-stitch along the pinned row to form the rod-pocket casing. Push the curtain rod through the top casing and ruche up the curtains to fit the rod.

TIP

To re-design these curtains for a traditional living room, simply choose a more appropriate fabric and change the style of the trim. There are many trim alternatives available—look out for bullion or looped fringes, gorgeous braid, flanged cords, or one of the many tassel combinations on the market.

VARIATION

Even with a conventional heading tape, a deep ruffle above the gathers gives a simple window a pretty, countrified look. The curtains have been made extra-long too, so that they fall in folds onto the floor, and frame the blue-painted window with its low sill.

Contrast-Top Tabbed Panels

A band of pretty floral fabric has been stitched to the top of this simple striped door panel, which is a great way to incorporate a small amount of expensive fabric into a room. The easy-to-make tabs along the top hang from a narrow rod that allows the panel to slide back for easy access to the door.

YOU WILL NEED

- Main decorator fabric—see right for estimating the yardage

- Contrast decorator fabric—see right for estimating the yardage

ESTIMATING YARDAGE

- Measure your window or door to determine the finished width and length of the curtain panel. (See page 186.) Take off 4 inches from the length measurement to allow for the tabs and add 4½ inches for the top and lower hems.

- To achieve the proper fullness, this heading needs fabric that measures one-and-a-half times the width of your door.

- Calculate how many tabs you will need along the top edge of the panel, spacing them approximately 4 inches apart. (See page 199.) For each tab allow a 4 x 9-inch strip of main fabric.

- Allow for a top facing from main fabric, the width calculated for the main panel by 2½ inches deep.

- For the contrast top band, allow a piece of contrast fabric the width calculated for the main panel, by the required depth plus 2½ inches for hems.

1 From the main fabric, cut out the required pieces for the main curtain panel and the top facing, and join the fabric lengths, if necessary, to form the finished panel widths. (See page 192). From the contrast fabric, cut out the top band, joining any fabric widths, as above, for the correct panel width. Press a ⅜-inch hem onto the wrong side, along one long edge of the contrast band, then press over another 1⅝ inches and machine-stitch the hem in place.

2 Lay out the main panel flat, right side up, and place the contrast band on top, right side up and raw top and side edges matching. Pin the contrast band in place around the top and side edges and along the machined hem line.

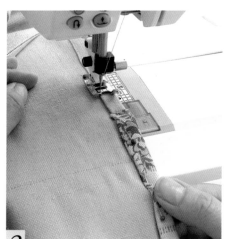

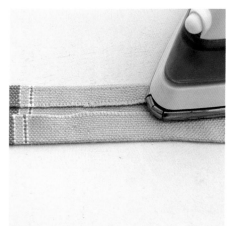

3 Press a ⅜-inch double-fold hem onto the wrong side, down both side edges of the panel, folding both fabrics together along the depth of the contrast band. Pin and machine-stitch the hems in place

4 Press a ⅝-inch hem onto the wrong side around all edges of the top facing.

5 Press a ⅝-inch hem onto the wrong side along the top edge of the main curtain panel, folding both fabrics together. Pin the hem in place.

TIP

When estimating the yardage, think carefully about how you are going to cut out your contrasting fabrics. In the main project, the two fabrics have been cut with the stripes running in different directions, horizontally and vertically, to add more visual excitement to the curtain panel. The tabs have been cut from the solid color running between the stripes.

VARIATION

Tabbed tops can be used on a Roman shade, too, but they are purely for decoration. The shade is made in the usual way. (See pages 132–137.) But it has extra tabs stitched along the top above the hook-and-loop tape. The shade is attached to the covered wooden lath, and the decorative tabs are slotted onto a pole fitted above.

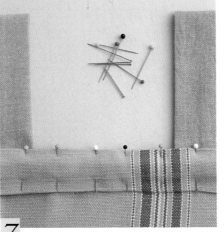

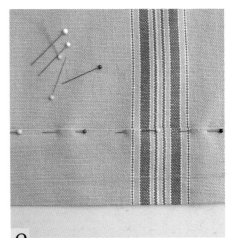

6 Cut out and make up the required number of tabs, as shown on page 199. Fold each tab in half with the center seam on the inside. With raw edges matching, pin each folded tab to the top hem of the panel, placing the first and last tab in line with the side edges of the panel. Space out the remaining tabs evenly. Pin and baste the tabs in place.

7 With wrong sides together, place the top facing along the top edge of the main panel, matching the pressed top and side edges, and sandwiching the tabs in-between. Pin and machine-stitch the facing in place around all the edges.

8 Press a 2-inch double-fold hem onto the wrong side along the lower edge of the main panel. Pin and machine-stitch the hem in place close to the inner pressed edge. To finish, slipstitch the open side edges of the lower hem together. (See page 190.)

SHEERS

Cuffed Panels

This panel of finely woven cotton fabric works well as a semi-sheer curtain. Give it a feminine folded-over top, with a decorative beaded trim, and you have the prettiest lightweight window treatment for a summer dining room. A rod-pocket heading, which encases the curtain rod, means there is no need to use bulky pleater tapes, keeping the look simple and uncluttered.

YOU WILL NEED

- Main decorator fabric—see right for estimating the yardage

- Matching sewing thread

- Small amount of iron-on interfacing

- Dressmakers' chalk

- Measuring tape or ruler

- Ready-made beaded trim—see right for estimating the yardage

ESTIMATING YARDAGE

- Measure your window to determine the finished width and length of the panels. (See page 186.) Add 12 inches to the length measurement for the cuff top, and 4 inches for the top and lower hems.

- To achieve the proper fullness, this heading needs fabric that measures one-and-a-half times the width of your window.

- The beaded trim should be as wide as the finished panel, plus 1 ⅛ inches for neatening the ends.

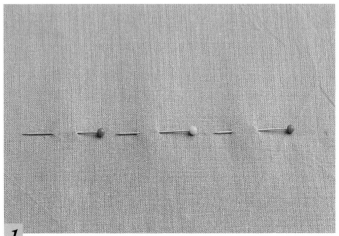

1 Cut out the required number of fabric lengths for each panel. Join the fabric lengths, if necessary, with flat fell seams to form the finished panel widths. (See page 193.) Lay one panel on a flat surface, wrong side up, and measure 12 inches down from the top edge. Mark across the panel width at this position with pins. Repeat with the remaining panel.

2 With the right side of the fabric facing up, press the cuffs along the pinned lines. Remove the pins.

3 Unfold one cuff, and with the panel facing wrong side up, mark 1½ inches down from the pressed line, on the main panel, with pins at both side edges. Carefully make a horizontal snip into each side edge, by no more than 1⅛ inches.

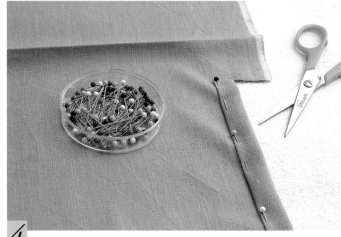

4 Press a ⅝-inch double-fold hem onto the wrong side below the snip, on the main panel. Pin and machine-stitch the side hems in place, stitching also across the top raw edge of each hem toward the snip position.

TIP

This panel should be made from a plain or reversible fabric, as the cuff is folded-back to reveal the wrong side of the fabric. If you want to use a non-reversible, or a patterned fabric, make a seam along the top-folded edge of the rod pocket. Then the cuff fabric can be turned over to show the right side.

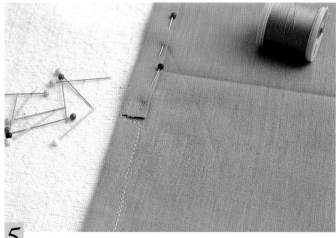

5 Turn the panel over so that the right side is facing up. Press a ⅝-inch double-fold hem to the right side above the snips. Pin and machine-stitch in place, stitching across the snipped raw edges as before.

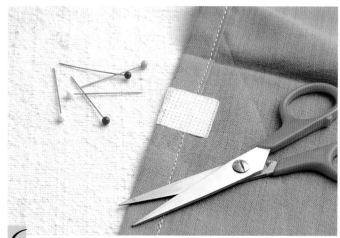

6 Cut two ¾ x ¾-inch squares of iron-on interfacing. Lay one piece over each snipped and stitched side hem, on the right side of the main panel. Press in place using a hot iron, to reinforce the side edges.

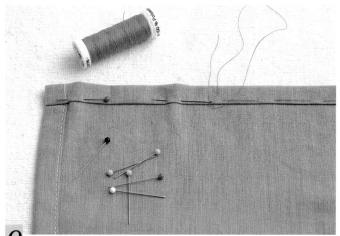

9 Press a ⅝-inch double-fold hem onto the wrong side of the cuff along the bottom edge. Pin and baste in place.

10 Lay one length of the beaded trim along the wrong side of the basted hem, aligning the tape edge with the pressed edge of the hem. Tuck under the raw cut ends of the tape to the wrong side. Pin and machine-stitch the tape in place, using a zipper foot on your machine. Remove the basting stitches. Repeat steps 3 to 10 with the remaining panel.

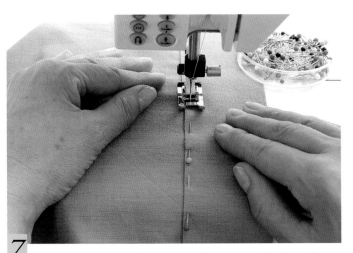

7 Press a 2-inch double-fold hem to the wrong side along the bottom edge of the main panel. Pin and machine-stitch in place close to the inner pressed edge.

8 With the cuff folded onto the right side of the panel, mark the rod-pocket position for the curtain rod, by lightly drawing a line 2 inches down from the top pressed edge, using the dressmakers' chalk and ruler. Pin and machine-stitch along the chalked line.

VARIATION

An alternative to stitching on a ready-made beaded strip is to hand-sew beads along the edge of a cuff panel. Make a small stitch in the panel edge and thread two or more beads onto the needle. Finish off by taking the thread round a tiny bead on the end, then push the needle back through the previous beads. Secure with a couple of tiny stitches.

Simple Draped Sheer

Take a tip from Scandinavian style. In northern parts of Scandinavia, as well as in Canada and Alaska, the winters are long and dark, and daylight is a precious commodity. People in these countries don't wrap their windows in heavy draperies, but lightly swathe rods with muslin or voile to let in maximum light. Even if you prefer full-length curtains for winter, it's a lovely idea to take down heavy curtains for the summer months and swag the bare rods with a length of fine muslin or silk. Add a touch of color to your draperies by winding around some fine red cord, too.

VARIATION

A simple swag doesn't have to be made from a length of fine muslin. Soften the appearance of a Roman shade with a drape of plain cotton fabric, elegantly swathed across a wooden pole and left to hang asymmetrically down the sides.

Scalloped Panel

Made from the softest drift of muslin with a subtle checkered weave, this sheer panel can be lowered to screen the entire window, or hooked up at the sides with ribbon loops to give a glimpse of the garden beyond. The pretty scalloped edge turns the simple panel into something special, creating focus for a plain window. Also see page 144 where this bathroom window panel is partnered with a Roman shade for an alternative look.

YOU WILL NEED

- Sheer decorator fabric—see right for estimating the yardage
- ⅛-inch wide ribbon for the side loops—see step 9 for estimating the yardage
- Matching sewing thread
- Paper for making a template
- Dressmakers' chalk
- Curtain hardware—PVC-coated wires, hooks, and eyes
- Wire cutters

ESTIMATING YARDAGE

- Measure your window to find the finished width and length of the panel. (See page 187.)
- Add 1½ inches to the width measurement for side hems, and 1¾ inches to the length measurement for the top hem and lower seam allowance.
- For the bottom facing, allow for a strip of fabric the width estimated for the main panel, by 8 inches deep.

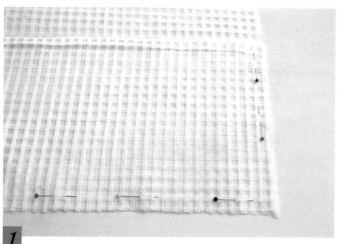

1 Cut out your panel and facing pieces, and join any fabric widths with flat fell seams if necessary to obtain the correct panel width. (See page 193.) Make a template for the scalloped edge, using the paper, as shown on page 201. Press a ⅝-inch hem onto the wrong side along the top edge of the facing, and, with right sides together, place the facing on top of the main panel along the lower edge, with raw edges even. Pin the pieces together.

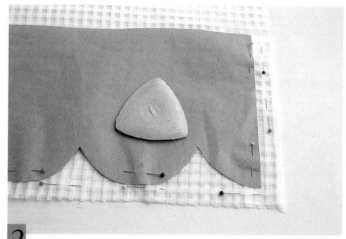

2 Lay the paper template on top of the facing, placing it ⅝ inch from the bottom edge and ¾ inch from the side edges. Pin in place. Using the dressmakers' chalk, trace around the scallop shapes and up both side edges of the template. Remove the template.

4 Cut out around the scallop shapes, leaving a ⅜-inch seam allowance. Clip notches into the curved seam allowances around each scallop and carefully snip into the seam allowance, close to the stitch line, between each scallop.

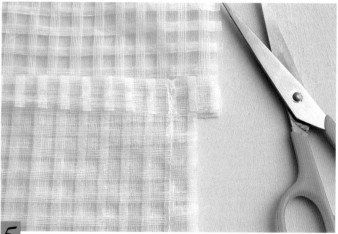

5 Trim away the seam allowances at each side of the panel to a depth of ⅜ inch, starting ⅝ inch below the top pressed edge of the facing, working down to the bottom scalloped edge.

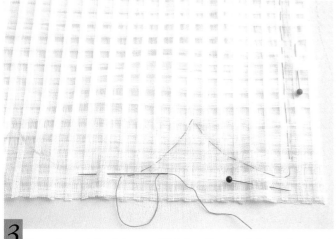

3 Baste through both layers of fabric, all around the scallops and along the side edges following the chalk lines. Machine-stitch the pieces together close to the basted line. Remove the basting stitches.

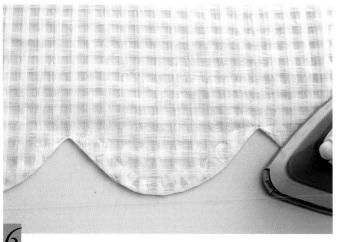

6 Turn the facing through to the right side, carefully easing out the corners and smoothing out the scalloped shapes with the point of a pair of scissors. Press the seamed edges flat.

TIPS

• Before starting any sewing project it is best to test and, if necessary, adjust the combination of needle, thread, and stitch length on your sewing machine. The general rule is that the finer the yarn in the fabric, the finer the needle. So for sheer fabrics, try a sharp-point needle, size 12 (80), with a synthetic thread and a small stitch length.

• When pressing, steam may cause soft sheers to pucker or shrink, so test a scrap first, and always use a light touch to avoid over-pressing. Crisp sheers are a lot easier to handle and rarely require any special pressing techniques.

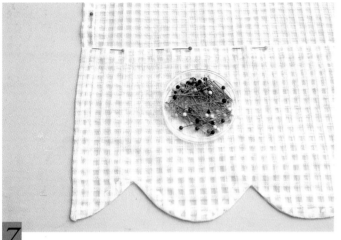

7 Press a ⅜-inch double-fold hem onto the wrong side along the remaining raw side edge of the panel, and pin in place. Pin the top pressed edge of the facing to the panel and machine-stitch it in place, close to the folded edge. Machine-stitch the side hems in place.

8 Press a ⅜-inch hem onto the wrong side along the top edge of the panel, then press over a ¾-inch hem. Pin and machine-stitch the hem in place close to the inner pressed edge.

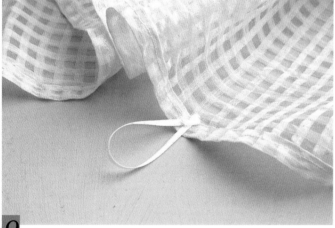

VARIATION

Sheer magic—a classic Roman shade brings a soft, diffused light to an elegant bedroom when made from fine, sheer fabric. The softness of the fabric needs narrow, transparent rods, so look in drapery stores for clear plastic ones, rather than using those made from solid wood.

9 Cut the ribbon into 4-inch lengths and fold each piece in half to form a loop. Lay the panel out flat, wrong side up. Pin the raw ends of each loop to the side edges of the panel, placing the top two loops 16½ inches from the top of the panel and the bottom two loops in line with the top of the facing. Space out the remaining ribbon loops equally, about 8 inches apart. Hand-stitch the ribbons in place. Thread the wire through the top hem. Screw the hooks into the frame and place one of the eyes over one hook. Stretch the wire and place the remaining eye over the corresponding hook.

Ribbon-Tied Shade

What could be prettier on a small window than a muslin panel that is rolled and tied with soft organza ribbons? Purely decorative, this translucent panel is best-suited to a window with a private view.

YOU WILL NEED

- Sheer decorator fabric—see right for estimating the yardage

- Hook-and-loop tape that is the width of the finished shade

- Matching sewing thread

- 1½-inch-wide organza ribbon—see right for estimating the yardage

- 1 x 2-inch wooden mounting board to fit the width of the finished shade

- Screws

ESTIMATING YARDAGE

- Prepare the wooden mounting board as shown on page 189, but ignore instructions for inserting the screw eyes.

- Measure your window to find the finished width and length of the shade. (See page 187.) Add 2¼ inches to the length and 1½ inches to the width measurements for hem allowance.

- For the organza ribbon, allow four times the length of the window.

1 Cut out the shade panel and press a ⅜-inch double-fold hem along each side edge. Pin and machine-stitch in place.

2 Press a ¾-inch double-fold hem along the lower edge of the panel. Pin and machine-stitch in place.

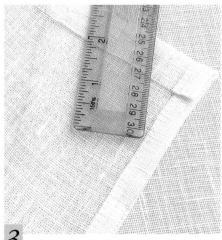

3 Press a ¾-inch hem along the top edge of the panel. Pin and machine-stitch in place.

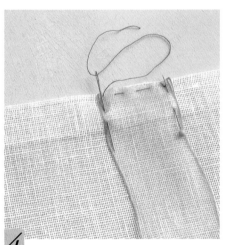

4 Cut the ribbon into four equal lengths and fold over a single-turned hem at one end of each length. Lay the shade panel flat, with the right side up, and pin the folded ends of two ribbons along the top edge, 4 inches from the side edges. Baste the ribbons in place in a box shape, following the lines of the top hem.

5 Machine-stitch the two ribbons in place following the basting stitches, then remove the basting stitches.

6 Turn the shade panel over. On the wrong side, pin the folded ends of the remaining two ribbons to the top hem, placing them ⅜ inch down from the top edge, at the same positions as the front ribbons. Baste in place.

TIPS

• To prevent the ribbon ties from fraying, cut a V into the bottom edges by folding the ribbon in half lengthways and cutting diagonally across, toward the fold line.

• Always use very sharp scissors when cutting ribbon, to achieve a neat, clean cut and to avoid pulling the weave out of shape.

7 Pin the fluffy side of the hook-and-loop tape to the wrong side of the shade along the top edge, enclosing the top of the ribbons. Machine-stitch the tape in place. Attach the panel to the wooden mounting board by pressing the two sides of the hook-and-loop tape together. Roll up the shade by hand to about halfway up the window, and tie the ribbons into bows.

VARIATION

Make this delightful window dressing in the same way as the ribbon-tied shade, but use a fine cotton fabric rather than a sheer one. The long ties are made of the same fabric, and hold the shade in place under the bottom hem with decorative bows. This panel has been pinned along the window frame, but you could fix it to a mounting board instead.

Cuff-Topped Muslins

A summer bedroom has been given a light and airy feel with ready-made muslin panels, bought on a vacation to India. Too beautiful to cut down, but too long for the window, the solution was to fold the tops over twice before hanging them from a rod with pincer clips, creating an interesting swag effect. These panels have a strong blue edging woven into the fabric, but it would be easy to appliqué ribbons to the edges of a plain muslin panel to create the same effect.

VARIATION

Light muslin panels will give any room a fresh, summery feel. A contrast-embroidered motif drifts dreamily against the light on these ready-made panels, and the color picks up on the shades of red used on the pillows.

Striped-Sheer Tabbed Panel

Take down thick, heavy curtains for the summer months, and replace them with sheer gossamer panels that will gently billow in the warm breezes. Here, one single panel has been made in striped voile, to pull across a set of French doors. If you wish, make a pair of panels for a conventional window treatment.

YOU WILL NEED

- Sheer decorator fabric—see right for estimating the yardage

- Matching sewing thread

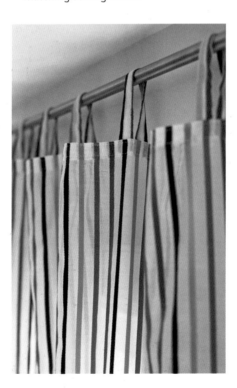

ESTIMATING YARDAGE

- Measure your window to determine the finished width and length of the panels. (See page 186.) Take 4 inches from the length measurement, to allow for the tabs, and add 7 inches for the top and bottom hems.

- To achieve the proper fullness, this heading needs fabric that measures one-and-a-half times the width of your window.

- Calculate how many tabs you will need along the top edge of the panel, spacing them approximately 8 inches apart. (See page 199.) For each tab allow a 4 x 10-inch strip.

1 Cut out the required number of fabric pieces and tabs for each curtain panel. Join the fabric lengths with French seams, if necessary, to form the finished panel widths. (See page 192.) With wrong sides facing, press each tab strip in half lengthways, and then press the long raw edges onto the wrong side, to meet down the center press line.

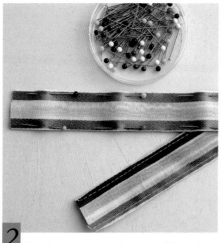

2 Pin the long pressed edges of the tabs together, and carefully machine-stitch down both long sides, working close to the edge. Remove the pins.

3 Press a ⅜-inch double-fold hem onto the wrong side, down both side edges of the fabric panel. Pin and machine-stitch in place.

5 Fold the top hem and loops 2 inches onto the wrong side of the panel and press in place.

6 Lay the panel on a flat surface, with the wrong side up, and the top edge facing away from you. Fold the top hem in half along its length, bringing the first pressed edge up, level with the top edge. The tabs will now face upward. Pin the top hem in place along both the top and bottom edges.

7 Machine-stitch the top hem in place, stitching close to the top edge, and sandwiching in the tabs. Work a second row of stitching ¾ inch below the first, removing the pins as you work. Remove the basting stitches.

4 Press a 1-inch hem onto the right side, along the top edge of the fabric panel. Fold a tab strip in half, and with raw edges even, pin it to the top hem, placing it up to the side edge, as shown. Repeat at the other end of the top hem with another tab, and space the remaining tabs evenly in-between. Baste in place.

8 Press a double-fold 2-inch hem onto the wrong side of the panel, at the bottom edge. Pin and machine-stitch the hem in place.

TIP

If you use a single piece of very sheer voile fabric for your panels, you can use the selvages, along the sides of the fabric, instead of turning over and machine-stitching the hems.

VARIATION

A sheer, unlined curtain held up to the light shows off delicate leaf shapes that have been appliquéd onto a contrast-colored panel. If you want to try your hand at some creative embroidery, make your own leaves; if not, buy ready-made sheer panels.

Swag-Draped Panel

The large oval window is such a beautiful and unusual feature of this bedroom, but not an easy shape to curtain. The solution: two wooden holdbacks, attached to the wall above each side of the window, draped with a pale sheer panel and trimmed with a delicate pom-pom edging. This house sits deep in the countryside, so privacy is not a problem for the owners. But if you need more cover or to block out the daylight, a simple roller shade could be fixed beneath the fabric.

VARIATION

Some windows are just too beautiful to curtain at all. A long, leaded window needs only a twig wreath and a bowl of pine cones for a special look.

Rod-Pocket Panels

There cannot be an easier way to dress a window than with these simple rod-pocket panels. They look pretty while filtering the light and adding privacy to a pair of country-style windows where there is not a lot of space. (Because these panels are fixed to the window itself they are not suitable for casement or sliding windows.)

YOU WILL NEED

- Main lightweight or sheer decorator fabric—see right for estimating yardage
- Matching sewing thread
- Curtain hardware—PVC-coated wires, hooks, and eyes
- Wire cutters
- Measuring tape or ruler

ESTIMATING YARDAGE

- Measure your window to find the finished width and length of the panels. (See page 186.) Add 4 inches to the length measurement for hems.
- For fullness, this heading needs one-and-a-half times the width of your window.
- For a pair of curtain panels divide the width measurement in two.

1 From the main fabric cut out your panels. Join fabric lengths, if necessary, to form the finished panel widths. (See page 192.) Press a ⅜-inch double-fold-hem to the wrong side, along both side edges of the panels.

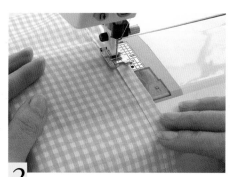

2 Pin and machine-stitch the hems in place, stitching close to the inner pressed edge.

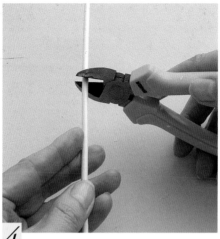

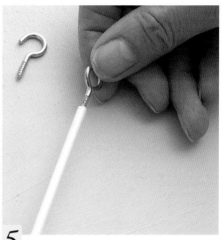

3 Press and then pin a 1-inch double-fold hem to the wrong side along both the top and lower edges of the panels. Machine stitch the hems in place, stitching close to the inner pressed edge. If desired, work a second row of machine stitching close to the top and bottom pressed edge, to form a tiny ruffle.

4 Using the wire cutters, cut the PVC-coated wire to four lengths, each 1½ inches shorter than the width of the window.

5 Carefully screw a circular eye into each end of the wires, as far as it will go.

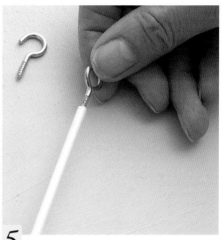

6 Thread the wires through the top hems, gathering the fabric to fit. Screw the hooks into the window frame and place one of the eyes over one hook. Stretch the wire and place the other eye over the corresponding hook. Repeat for the base hems with the remaining wires and hooks.

Give a pair of long, deep windows a European feel using a slight variation on the curtains featured in the main project. They are made in exactly the same way, but the slightly different appearance is provided by simple fabric ties that gather the curtains together low down on the window.

TIPS

• If using a sheer fabric, look out for special curtain rods made from clear or translucent plastic on which to hang your panels.

• Another stronger alternative to wires are sash rods. These use shallow mounting brackets so the window treatments hang close to the glass.

• Both types of curtain rods are available from good drapery stores.

123

SHADES

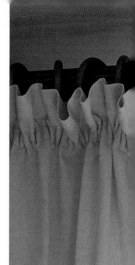

Unlined Swedish Shade

This traditional Scandinavian shade is one of the simplest shades to make and ideal for a beginner. Because it is a roll-up shade, it works particularly well if you make it in gingham check fabric that looks great from both sides.

YOU WILL NEED

- Main decorator fabric—see right for estimating the yardage

- Matching sewing thread

- Fine Roman shade cord, or jute string

- 1½ x ¾-inch wooden slat to fit the width of the shade

- Small piece of thin leather or narrow fabric ties. (See step 2 on page 198.)

- Two brass curtain rings

- Bradawl

- Leather hole punch

- One ⅜-inch diameter dowel rod to fit the width of the shade, less ¾ inch

- Two 1½-inch-long brass screws

- A wooden drapery pull and brass cleat

ESTIMATING YARDAGE

- Measure your window to determine the finished width and length of the shade. (See page 187.)

- Add 7 inches to the length measurement and 2½ inches to the width measurement for hem allowances.

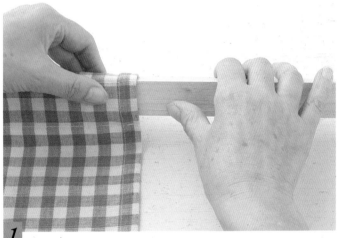

1 Cut out the required number of fabric lengths, and join the widths together, if necessary, with flat fell seams to form the finished panel width. (See page 193.) Press a double-fold ⅝-inch hem down each side edge of the shade panel, and machine-stitch in place. Press a double-fold 1-inch hem along the lower edge, pin, and machine-stitch in place. Press a 2½-inch double-fold hem along the top edge, pin, and machine-stitch in place. Insert the lath through the top hem casing.

2 Cut two ⅝ x 8-inch leather strips, or make two narrow fabric ties, to attach the brass curtain rings.

5 Push the screws through the holes in the leather strips or ties, and then through the wooden slat, until they appear out through the back. You will use the screws to secure the shade operating cord (or jute string).

6 Insert the length of dowel rod into the bottom hem, and slipstitch the ends of the hem closed, encasing the dowel rod. (See page 190.)

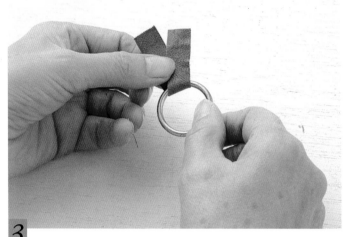

3 Thread a curtain ring onto each of the leather strips or fabric ties, and fold the strips in half across their width, so that the ring sits in the fold at the center.

4 Position the leather strips or ties 6 inches from the side edges of the shade, along the top channel containing the slat. Use a bradawl to make a pilot hole through both layers of the leather strips or ties and the shade fabric. Remove the leather strips or ties and drill a hole right through the slat at each position for the screws. Using the leather hole punch, make the holes in the ends of the leather strips or ties at the bradawl marks.

TIP

To keep the Swedish shade tightly rolled, let it unroll completely and then roll it up again by hand for a few turns, before pulling up the cord to support it.

7 Lay the shade on a flat surface with the wrong side up. Make a loop in one end of the shade cord (or jute string). Thread the loop over the projecting end of the right-hand screw and pull it up tight to secure.

8 To create the operating mechanism, thread the shade by bringing the cord down the wrong side of the shade and under the bottom edge. Turn the shade to the right side. Now bring the cord up the right side and through the first curtain ring. Pass the cord across the top edge of the shade and make a long loop in the free end. Thread the loop through the second ring and bring the free end back down the shade to the lower edge.

9 Complete the threading by taking the cord under the bottom edge. Turn the shade over once again, and take the cord up the wrong side to the second screw. Make a loop in the end and attach it firmly to the screw.

10 Attach the slat to the wall with the screws. Attach the drapery pull to the long loop at the front of the shade, and fix the cleat to the side of the window frame. Roll up the shade, by hand, and secure it at your selected position by winding the cord around the cleat.

A simple shade like this one doesn't have to be used on the window. Use the same fabric and make a matching shade for covering a set of open storage shelves in a child's bedroom. It will roll up and down easily, and will make a world of difference when it comes to tidying up the toys and games at bedtime.

Unlined Roman Shade

Make a simple unlined shade to filter light at a kitchen or bathroom window. With only straight seams to sew, this project is easy enough for a complete beginner. Partner the shade with simple curtains in a coordinating fabric.

YOU WILL NEED

- Main decorator fabric—see right for estimating the yardage

- Hook-and-loop tape the width of the finished shade

- Roman shade tape (this is like tubing, with a casing running along the center and thread loops attached—if you are unable to find this type of tape at your local drapery store, see the tip on the next page)

- Matching sewing thread

- 1 x 2-inch wooden mounting board to fit the width of the finished shade

- Brass screw eyes

- Dressmakers' chalk

- Measuring ruler

- Dowel rods ⅜ inch in diameter to measure 1½ inches less than the width of the finished shade

- Thin wooden slat to measure 1½ inches less than the width of the finished shade

- Fine Roman shade cord

- A bodkin

- A drapery pull and brass cleat

- Fixing screws or angle irons

ESTIMATING YARDAGE

- Prepare the mounting board. (See page 189.)

- Measure your window to determine the finished width and length of the shade. (See page 187.) Add 4¾ inches to the length and width for hem allowances.

1 Cut out the required number of fabric lengths and join the widths together, if necessary, to form the finished shade panel, using flat fell seams. (See page 193.) Press a 1⅛-inch double-fold hem down each long side edge of the fabric panel, pin, and machine-stitch in place.

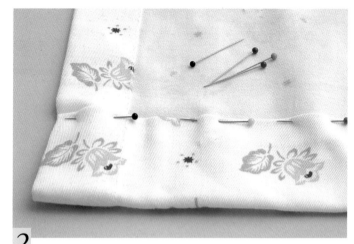

2 Press a 2-inch double-fold hem along the lower edge of the panel, pin, and machine-stitch in place.

3 Measure the finished length of the shade from the lower edge. Mark the position of the top edge with pins. Press the top hem to the wrong side along the pin-line. Trim the hem allowance to ⅝ inch and pin in place. Pin the fluffy side of the hook-and-loop tape to the wrong side of the shade at the top, enclosing the raw edge. Machine-stitch the tape in place.

4 Calculate the spacing positions for the Roman shade tape. (See page 187.) Working on the wrong side of the shade, mark the spacing positions with pins along each side hem. Lightly draw horizontal lines across the shade, joining the pins, using the dressmakers' chalk and ruler.

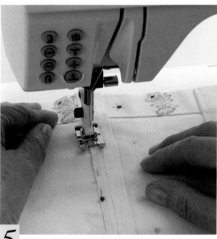

5 Cut lengths of Roman shade tape to fit the width of the finished shade, plus 1⅛ inches. Place the tapes on the shade, positioning the top edge of each piece along the chalked lines. Machine-stitch the tapes in place along the top edge, starting and finishing ¾ inch from the edge. Make sure that all the loops are aligned.

6 Insert the dowel rods through the casing in the Roman shade tape, and the wooden slat through the casing in the lower hem. Slipstitch the open ends of the hem closed. To neaten the raw ends of the Roman shade tape, fold over a double-fold hem at each end, and catchstitch to secure. (See page 191.)

7 Lay the shade, wrong side up, on a flat surface. On the Roman shade, measure and mark with pins vertical rows, placing the first and last rows 1 inch in from the side edges. The remaining vertical rows should be evenly spaced across the center of the shade. Tie a length of the fine cord, through the loop in the bottom strip of Roman shade tape, at the first pin position.

8 Using a bodkin, thread the cord up vertically through the tape loops at the pin positions. Repeat steps 7 and 8, threading cord up the remaining vertical rows. Continue making the shade as shown in step 9 of the Lined Roman Shade. (See page 142.) Fit the shade to the window following the instructions in the tip box on page 142.

TIPS

• This type of shade is best made from one piece of fabric. However, if you need to join fabric widths in order to obtain the correct width, allow for a full width to be placed centrally, with half-widths (of equal dimensions) stitched down each side.

• If you cannot find the type of Roman shade tape shown in these instructions, then make your own casings. Follow the instructions for making the shade up to and including step 4. Then cut out a straight-grain strip of fabric for each shade tape position, 2¾ inches wide, by the finished width of the shade.

With wrong sides together, fold each strip in half along its length, bringing the long side edges together, and press flat. Machine-stitch the long edges together with a ¼-inch seam allowance. Using the stitch line as a guide press a ¼-inch double-fold hem to one side along the long edge and machine-stitch the hem in place.

Continue making the shade following steps 5 and 6, using the casings you have made rather than the tapes and placing the long pressed edge (not the hemmed edge) up to the chalk lines.

Continue making the shade following steps 8 and 9 of the "Lined Roman Shade," on page 142.

VARIATION

The simplest decoration is often the best, and suits an understated room. This unlined Roman shade has been given a narrow, contrasting trim along the lower edge, stitched and bound for just a hint of color. The blue of the trim picks up the sprig pattern of the main fabric to emphasize the accent color.

Lined Roman Shade

This classic shade will look chic and contemporary in a modern room, or will sit neatly behind simple panels. The fabric used here is embellished with pretty ribbon roses, adding a sweet decorative touch. See page 22 for instructions for the accompanying curtains.

YOU WILL NEED

- Main decorator fabric—see right for yardage

- Drapery lining—see right for yardage

- Hook-and-loop tape the width of the finished shade

- Small plastic Roman shade rings

- Matching thread

- 2 x 1-inch mounting board to fit the width of the window

- Brass screw eyes

- Dressmakers' chalk

- Measuring ruler

- Dowel rods ⅜-inch diameter to measure 1¼ inches less than the width of the finished shade

- Thin wooden slat to measure 1½ inches less than the width of the finished shade

- Fine Roman shade cord, a drapery pull, and a cleat

- Fixing screws or angle irons

ESTIMATING YARDAGE

- Prepare the mounting board. (See page 189.)

- Measure your window to determine the finished width and length of the shade. (See page 187.)

- For the main fabric, add 2½ inches to the width measurement and 3⅛ inches to the length measurement for hem allowances.

- The lining needs to be the finished width measurement of the shade, by the cut length measurement, but add 1¼ inches extra to the length for every dowel rod casing required. (See page 187.)

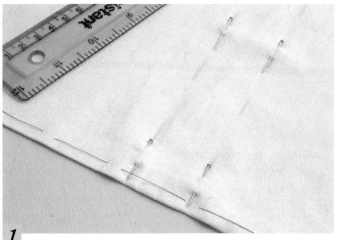

1 Cut out the required number of main fabric and lining lengths. Join the widths together, if necessary, to form the finished shade widths. (See page 192.) Press a ⅝-inch hem down each side of the lining and baste in place. Calculate the spacing between the casing fold lines. (See page 187.) On the right side of the lining, mark the fold lines with pins, and then lightly draw the lines using the dressmakers' chalk and ruler.

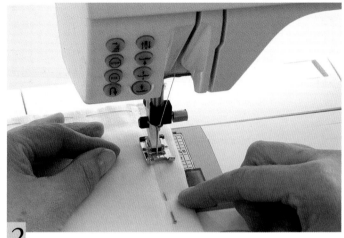

2 Fold the lining panel along each marked line and press. Pin and machine-stitch ⅝ inch from each fold line to form the casings for the dowel rods. Press a 1¼-inch hem to the wrong side down each side edge of the main shade. Pin and baste in place. Lay the main shade panel on a flat surface with the wrong side up.

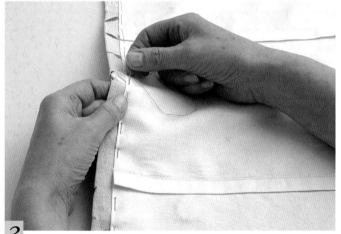

3 With wrong sides together, place the lining on top of the shade panel with the top edges matching and the main fabric showing ⅝-inch either side of the lining. Pin the lining to the shade panel along the side edges. Baste and slipstitch the side edges in place. Remove the basting stitches and press. (See page 190.)

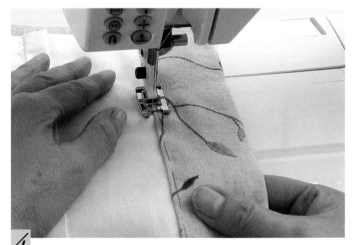

4 Press a ⅜-inch hem to the wrong side, along the lower edge of the shade, then press over a 2-inch hem. Pin, baste, and machine-stitch in place. Remove the basting stitches.

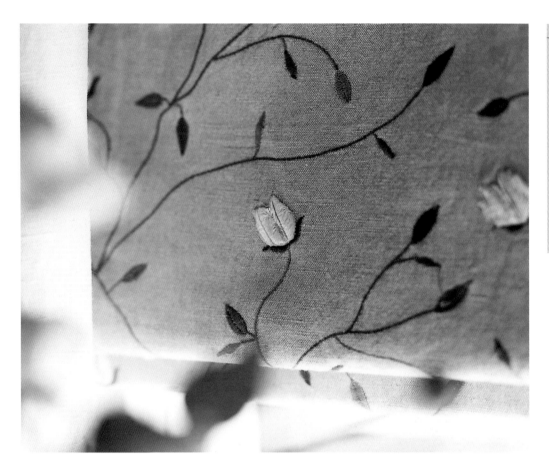

TIP

For a professional finish, ensure that the rings are accurately placed in perfect vertical rows so the shade will draw up evenly.

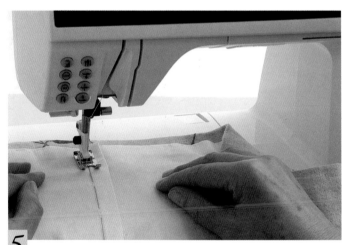

5 Pin, baste, and machine-stitch the lining and main shade fabric together across the shade, following the first rod casing stitch line and making sure to keep both layers of the fabric flat. Repeat this step, working up the length of the shade, from the bottom casing to the top.

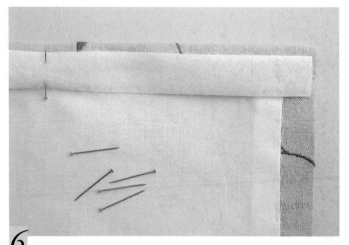

6 Measure the finished length of the shade from the lower edge and mark the top edge of the shade with pins. Press the top hem to the wrong side along the pin line. Trim the hem allowance to ⅝ inch. Pin the fluffy side of the hook-and-loop tape to the wrong side of the shade at the top, enclosing the raw edge. Machine stitch the tape in place.

7 Insert the dowel rods through the open ends of each casing and insert the wooden slat through the bottom hem casing. Slipstitch the open ends of the casings and hem edges closed. (See page 190.)

8 Lay the shade on a flat surface with the lining facing up. Measure and mark the positions of the rings on the casings. The first and last vertical rows of the rings should be 2 inches in from the side edges. The remaining vertical rows should be evenly spaced across the center of the shade. Hand-stitch all the rings in place.

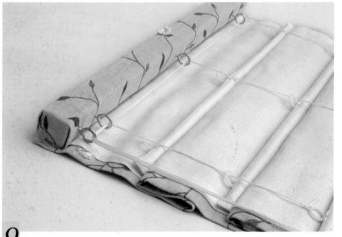

9 Fasten the shade to the mounting board using the hook-and-loop tape. Tie the Roman shade cord to the bottom ring of the first vertical row; thread it up through the remaining rings and then through the screw eyes in the lath, to the side of the blind where the draw cords will be situated. Repeat, threading each vertical row of the rings. Knot the cord about 20 inches from the ends, then attach the drapery pull to the ends.

TIP

To fit the shade above the window, open the hook-and-loop tape as far as the pilot holes. (There is no need to remove the shade totally from the lath.) Screw the lath to the wall or window frame through the pilot holes, then reattach the sides of the shade along the mounting board. Install a cleat on the wall or window frame, positioning it on the same side as the draw cords, to secure the cords when the shade is raised.

VARIATION

Make a set of Roman shades in a vibrantly colored, checked fabric to give a contemporary feel to a living room. Make the shades in varying widths to fit unconventional windows—this idea works well in a bay window too.

Relaxed Roman Shade

This is one of the easiest shades to make because there is no need for channels or tapes. The cord is threaded through small rings that have been hand-sewn into the edges. When lifted, the shade falls into soft folds, giving it an unstructured look. The sheer panel is featured on page 102.

YOU WILL NEED

- Main decorator fabric—see right for estimating the yardage

- Hook-and-loop tape the width of the finished shade

- Matching sewing thread

- 2 x 1-inch mounting board to fit the width of the finished shade

- Screw eyes

- A dowel rod ⅜ inch in diameter, to measure 1½ inches less than the width of the finished shade

- Fine Roman shade cord

- Small plastic Roman shade rings—two for each fold

- A drapery pull and awning cleat

- Screws

ESTIMATING YARDAGE

- Prepare the mounting board as shown on page 189.

- Measure your window to find the finished width and length of the shade. (See page 187.) Add 2⅜ inches to the length measurement, and 1½ inches to the width measurement for hem allowances.

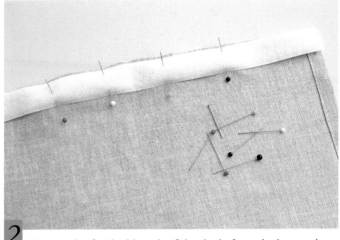

1 Cut out the required number of fabric lengths. Join the widths together, if necessary, to form the finished shade panel, using flat fell seams. (See page 193.) Press down a ⅜-inch double-fold hem on each long side edge of the fabric panel, pin, and machine-stitch the hems in place. Press a ¾-inch double-fold hem along the lower edge of the panel, pin, and machine-stitch in place.

2 Measure the finished length of the shade from the lower edge, and mark the position of the top edge with pins. Press the top hem onto the wrong side along the pin line. Trim the hem allowance to ⅝ inch and pin in place. Pin the loop side of the hook-and-loop tape onto the wrong side of the shade at the top, enclosing the raw hem edge. Machine-stitch the tape in place.

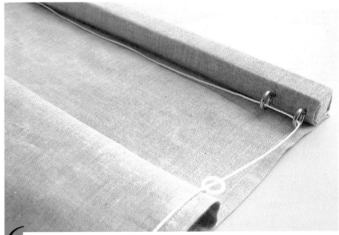

5 Lay the shade wrong side up on a flat surface. Tie a length of the fine cord through the ring at the bottom right and thread the cord up vertically through the remaining rings.

6 Repeat the knotting and threading of the cord through the set of rings on the left side of the shade. Continue making the shade as shown in step 9 of the Lined Roman Shade, on page 142. Fit the shade following the instructions in the tip box on page 142.

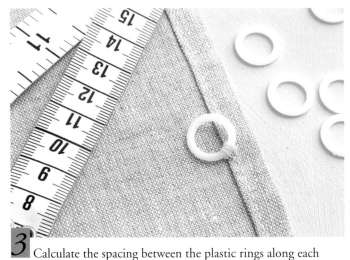

3 Calculate the spacing between the plastic rings along each side hem, and mark the positions with pins. (See page 187.) Oversew each in place. (See page 190.)

4 Insert the dowel rod through the channel in the bottom hem of the shade and neatly close the open ends with a hand slipstitch. (See page 190.)

TIP

This style of window shade is best made in a soft fabric, such as linen, but it also looks great in sheer and semi-transparent fabrics. If you are using sheer fabric, pair it with transparent plastic dowel rods which are designed specially for such use.

VARIATION

A contrast-colored border looks good with this type of shade, too. Here, off-white textured linen has been partnered with a rich, wine-red border along the two sides. Use fabrics of the same weight. Join the border fabric to the main panel before following the instructions for the main project.

147

Lined Swedish Shade

A ready-made patchwork fabric has been backed with cotton denim for an informal blind at a kitchen window. The construction is similar to making an unlined Swedish shade, but the lining folds around to the front to form a contrasting broad edging.

YOU WILL NEED

- Ready-made patchwork fabric—see right for estimating the yardage

- Contrast backing fabric—see right for estimating the yardage

- Matching sewing thread

- Fine Roman shade cord

- ¾-x-1½-inch mounting board to fit the finished width of the shade

- Small piece of thin leather

- Two brass curtain rings

- Bradawl

- Leather hole punch

- One dowel rod ⅜-inch diameter to fit the width of the shade, less ¾ inch

- Two 1½-inch long brass screws

- A drapery pull and brass cleat

ESTIMATING YARDAGE

- Measure your window to determine the finished width and length of the shade. (See page 187.)

- For the main patchwork fabric, take off 2¾ inches from the width measurement, and 1⅜ inches from the length measurement.

- For the contrast backing fabric, add 5⅛ inches to the finished width measurement, and 4 inches to the length measurement.

1 Cut out the required number of fabric lengths, and join the widths together, if necessary, with flat fell seams, to form the finished panel width. (See page 193.) With the wrong side up, lay the contrast backing fabric out flat. Place the main fabric in the center on top, with wrong sides together, leaving side borders of 4 inches, a top border of 3 inches, and a lower border of 2 inches.

2 Pin and baste the two layers of fabric together from top to bottom, following the lines of the patchwork fabric.

5 Machine-stitch the side borders in place, stitching close to the inner pressed edge, removing the pins as you work.

6 Press a ⅝-inch hem onto the wrong side along the top edge of the shade, and pin in place.

3 Press a ⅝-inch hem onto the wrong side along both side edges of the backing fabric.

4 To form the side borders, press the side edges over 2 inches onto the right side, down both side edges of the shade, and pin in place.

7 Press a top border of 1½ inches onto the right side of the shade along the top edge, pin, and machine-stitch in place close to the inner pressed edge.

8 Press a ⅝-inch hem onto the wrong side along the lower edge of the shade, then press over another 1 inch to form the lower border. Pin and machine-stitch the border in place close to the inner pressed edge. Insert the dowel through the bottom hem.

9 Slipstitch the open ends of the lower border, encasing the dowel rod. (See page 190.) Remove all the basting stitches.

10 Insert the mounting board through the top border, then continue to assemble and hang the shade as shown for the Unlined Swedish Shade on pages 128–130, following steps 2, 3, 4, 5, 7, 8, 9, and 10.

TIP

For a more structured-looking shade, use a heavier-weight linen or decorator fabric for both the main and the contrast-backing fabrics.

VARIATION

A more structured blind can be made if you choose fabrics that have plenty of body, like these printed linens. Used edge-to-edge, they won't need stitching through to hold them together, and the contrasting patterns are seen to best advantage when they coordinate with a matching fabric-covered cornice.

ACCESSORIES

Soft Cornice

Give a tall window a sense of balance and proportion by making a smart fabric-covered cornice that hides the curtain hardware. This type of cornice is most suitable for rooms with high ceilings, as it will appear to shorten the height of the window. Match the fabric used for the cornice to that used in the drapes for a unified look. (See page 44 for the panel instructions.)

YOU WILL NEED

- Main decorator fabric—see right for estimating the yardage

- Drapery lining—see right for estimating the yardage

- Bump interlining—see right for estimating the yardage

- 12-inch-wide double-sided, self-adhesive cornice stiffener

- Matching sewing thread

- Self-adhesive hook-and-loop tape

- Cornice mounting boar. (See page 189.)

- Angle irons

- Staple gun and staples

- Measuring ruler

- Dressmakers' chalk

ESTIMATING YARDAGE

- Prepare a wooden mounting board as shown on page 189, and fix in place with the angle irons. Measure along the front and the two side edges (the returns) of the mounting board, to find the width of the finished cornice.

- To find the depth of the cornice, divide the finished length of your panels, from track to floor, by six.

- Cut out a piece of self-adhesive cornice stiffener to the measurements calculated.

- Use the stiffener to work out your yardage. You will need enough fabric to cover the stiffener, plus ¾ inch for hems all around. The lining and interlining yardage will be the exactly the same size as the stiffener.

1 Stick the hook side of the hook-and-loop tape to the front edge and along the two returns of the mounting board and fix securely in place with the staple gun. From the main fabric, lining, and interlining, cut out all the pieces for the cornice. Join the fabric, lining, and interlining if necessary, to obtain your correct cornice width. (See page 192.) On a flat surface, lift the backing paper away from one side of the stiffener, and press the interlining down evenly along the full length as you remove the backing. Make sure the edges line up accurately.

2 Lay the main fabric piece wrong side uppermost on a flat surface, and using the ruler and dressmakers' chalk, draw a line ¾ inch in from the edges all around the fabric.

4 Snip away the corners of the fabric diagonally, then carefully peel the backing paper away from the other side of the stiffener. Turn over the ¾-inch hem allowance along the side edges and press down to attach the fabric to the self-adhesive surface.

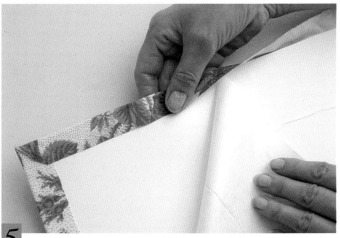

5 Turn over the ¾-inch hem allowance along the top and bottom edges, and press down to attach the fabric to the self-adhesive surface.

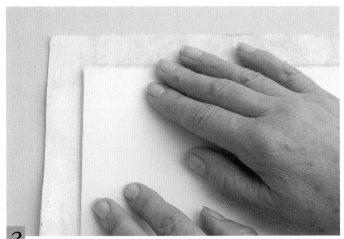

3 Lay the stiffener on top of the fabric, with the interlining side facing down, placing it between the chalk marks, thus leaving ¾ inch all around.

6 Press a ⅜-inch hem to the wrong side along each edge of the lining.

TIP

When attaching the fabrics to the self-adhesive stiffener, roll the fabrics up first, then gradually unroll them across the sticky surface, as you peel away the paper backing. This will help to keep the fabrics flat, without any creases or bumps.

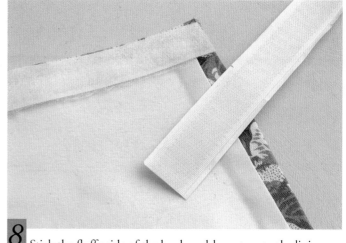

7 On a flat surface, lay the covered stiffener wrong (sticky) side uppermost. Carefully lay the lining centrally on top, with the right side up, and press down to attach the lining to the self-adhesive surface. Hand slipstitch the lining to the main fabric around all edges.(See page 190.)

8 Stick the fluffy side of the hook-and-loop tape to the lining side of the cornice along the top edge.

9 Make a sharp crease in the cornice, to fit along the returns of the mounting board, by folding in the sides and pressing them with an iron. Attach the cornice to the mounting board by pressing the two sides of the hook-and-loop tape together.

VARIATIONS

Right: A beautiful fabric is shown off to its best advantage when used to cover a deep, shaped pelmet. The dramatic shape of this scalloped pelmet makes the perfect foil for the long drapes made in the same design. Think carefully about the placing of the pattern when making a shaped pelmet, and draw out the shapes to fit around any repeating designs.

Left: Here a deep cornice has been made with the fabric's pattern running horizontally across the top of long drapes in which the pattern is used vertically. Extra texture is provided by pleating the fabric on the cornice. This has the effect of making the cornice appear wider than if the fabric pattern had been used vertically.

Gathered Valance

Soften the top of a pair of curtains with a gently gathered fabric valance. When combining a valance and panels with a strong pattern, as featured here, make them to the same fullness and coordinate the direction of the pattern.

YOU WILL NEED

- Main decorator fabric—see right for estimating the yardage

- Drapery lining—see right for estimating the yardage

- Narrow two-cord pleater tape—the width of the finished valance panel, plus 4 inches

- Matching sewing thread

- Hook-and-loop tape to fit the width of the gathered-up valance panel, plus 4 inches

- Valance mounting board. (See page 189.)

- Angle irons

- Staple gun and staples

ESTIMATING YARDAGE

- Prepare a wooden mounting board as shown on page 189, and fix in place with the angle irons.

- Measure along the front and the two side edges (the returns) of the mounting board to find the finished gathered width of the valance. The starting size of the valance panel needs to be twice this measurement, plus 1¼ inches extra for the hems each side. (You may need to join fabric lengths to obtain the correct width.)

- To find the depth of the valance panel, measure the height of your window from the floor to the underside of the mounting board, and divide this measurement by six. Add 3½ inches for the top and bottom hems.

- The lining should be the same width as the main fabric, but 2¾ inches shorter.

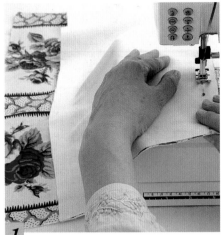

1 From the main fabric and lining cut out the pieces for the valance. Join fabric and lining widths to obtain the correct valance panel width. (See page 192.) Right sides together, lay the lining on top of the main fabric, with the lower edges even and the seams matching. Pin and machine-stitch the pieces together with a ⅝-inch seam along the bottom edge. Press open the seam.

2 With the wrong sides together, fold the lining on top of the main fabric, matching the raw edges at the top and the sides. Very lightly press the folded edge, so a strip of main fabric shows along the lower edge of the lining.

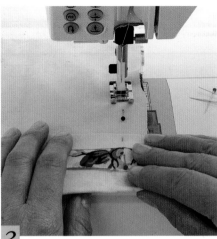

3 Refold the valance with the right sides together. Making sure the top edges of the main fabric and the lining are even, pin and machine-stitch a ⅜-inch seam down both short sides of the valance panel.

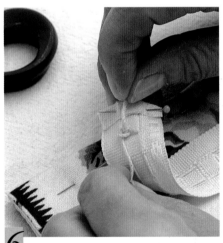

6 Cut the tape to fit the panel width, plus 4 inches. Pull the cords out to the wrong side, 2 inches from each end of the tape; knot the cord ends together at one end. Lay the panel on a flat surface, wrong side up. Place the tape 1 inch down from the pressed top edge, covering the raw edges, and leaving 2 inches extending at both sides. Pin in place.

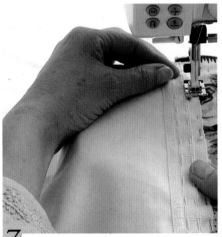

7 Trim away excess tape at both ends, leaving ¾ inch to fold under, in line with the edges of the panel. Pin in place. Machine-stitch the tape in place, stitching up one short end, along the top edge, and finishing at the base of the opposite short end. Make sure you leave the loose cord ends free. Machine-stitch the lower edge of the tape in place and remove all the pins.

8 Pull up the tape cords to gather the valance to fit the mounting board. Knot the free cord ends together. Evenly space the gathers along the length of the valance.

4 Turn the valance panel right side out. Baste the top raw edges together, then press the seamed side edges and the lower folded edge flat.

5 Press the top edge of the valance panel 1½ inches to the wrong side. Pin in place. Slipstitch the open side edges of the hem together. (See page 190.)

TIP

A valance panel can also be hung from a valance track, a drapery rod, or pole. However, remember that there is no need to allow for returns on a rod or pole, so the valance will use a little less fabric.

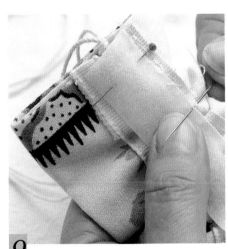

9 Pin the loop side of the hook-and-loop tape to the heading tape, and hand-stitch in place using oversew stitch along all edges. (See page 190.) Trim the ends of the cords. Staple the hook side of the hook-and-loop tape to the front and returns of the mounting board. Fix the valance panel in place by pressing the two sides of the hook-and-loop tape together.

VARIATION

A simple way to give a long pair of curtains a gathered, country look without making a separate valance, is to stitch a panel of fabric to the top, allowing it to fall over at the front and gather with the curtains as they are drawn back.

Zigzag Panel Valance

This is such a simple idea. Make a panel valance with an interesting zigzag shape and hang it from a rod with clip-rings. This is a style used everywhere in Scandinavian countries. It makes a charming treatment for a window with a café curtain.

YOU WILL NEED

- Main decorator fabric—see right for estimating the yardage

- Matching sewing thread

- Paper for making a pattern

- Dressmakers' chalk

- Clip-rings

ESTIMATING YARDAGE

- Decide on the finished depth of the valance panel—a good guide is to divide the height of the window, from the sill to the top of the pole, by six. Add 1¼ inches to the depth measurement for seam allowances at the top and lower edges.

- To achieve the proper fullness, this panel needs fabric that measures about one-and-a-quarter to one-and-a-half times the width of the window.

- Allow enough fabric to cut two valance panels to the measurements calculated.

1 To make a pattern, draw out the calculated depth and width of the valance panel on paper and cut out. Draw a parallel line 4 inches from the lower edge of the valance pattern, and divide the line (the width measurement) into equal sections, approximately 8 inches wide. Mark the positions on the line with pencil. Mark points along the bottom edge of the pattern spacing them halfway between the other points. Join the marks with diagonal lines to form the zigzag shape. Cut out the pattern along the zigzag line.

2 Cut out two fabric valance panels and join any fabric widths, if necessary, to obtain the correct valance width. Place the two valance panels together, with right sides facing, and lay the paper pattern on top. Draw around the lower zigzag edge using the dressmakers' chalk.

4 Machine-stitch around the pinned edges following the chalked lines, leaving the top edges open. When stitching the points, leave the machine needle down in the fabric, lift the presser foot, and turn the fabric. Replace the presser foot, and continue stitching to the next point.

5 Trim away the seam allowances at each downward point, no closer than ⅛ inch from the stitching line. Clip into the upward points, no closer than ⅛ inch from the stitching line.

6 Turn the valance panel right side out, carefully pushing the points with the end of a pair of scissors. Press the seamed edges flat.

3 Remove the pattern, and cut out the shaped bottom edge. Mark the seam allowances with dressmakers' chalk, ⅝ inch from the side and lower zigzag edges. Pin the fabric pieces together, leaving the top edges open.

7 Fold and press the top raw edges of the valance ⅝ inch onto the wrong side. Pin the pressed edges together. Slipstitch the top edges together. (See page 190.) Use clip-rings to attach the top of the finished valance to the curtain rod.

TIP

If you are unable to find clip-rings, oversew a set of standard curtain-rod rings, spaced evenly along the top edge of the valance panel. (See page 190.) Remove them for laundering.

VARIATION

The variety of colors and patterns in this child's bedroom make it a fantasy wonderland that will encourage creativity and play. A zigzag pelmet with tassels is made in the same way as the Soft Cornice for a more formal heading to a pair of long drapes. (See page 156.)

Upholstered Cornice

This pretty cornice is made using traditional upholstery techniques to cover a box frame with fabric. To add interest, the lower edge has been shaped into scallops, which works well with a simple roll-up shade. However, if the cornice will be used with formal draperies, keep the lower edge straight.

YOU WILL NEED

- Main decorator fabric—see right for estimating the yardage
- Contrast fabric for the lining—see right for estimating the yardage
- Lightweight batting or bump interlining—see right for estimating the yardage
- Medium-sized cable cord—see right for estimating the yardage
- Matching sewing thread
- Sheet of ⅜-inch thick MDF (medium-density fiberboard) or plywood
- Angle irons
- A curved upholstery needle
- Fabric adhesive
- Paper for making a template
- A staple gun, jigsaw, and drill
- Flat-head screws

ESTIMATING YARDAGE

- Measure your window to determine the length of your cornice and decide on the finished depth. As a general rule, the depth is approximately ⅙ the length of your shade or curtain.
- MDF or plywood cut into four pieces for the cornice box frame: one front piece to the length measured, by the depth calculated (plus 1½ inches for a shaped lower edge); one top piece 6-inches wide by the length of the cornice; and two side panels to the finished depth minus ⅜ inch, by the width minus ⅜ inch.
- For the main fabric, add the length of the cornice plus 12 inches—the width of the two side panels—and allow for a piece of fabric to this measurement, by the depth, adding ⅝ inch to all edges for hems.
- For the contrast lining, you will need the same yardage as the main fabric, but add ¾ inch all around for hems.
- For the cable cord, allow enough to fit around the lower edge of the cornice box frame.
- For covering the cable cord, first gauge the width of your fabric strip. To do this, measure around the cord and allow an extra 1¼ inches for seam allowances. Allow for enough straight-grain strips of contrast fabric, of this width, to fit the length of your cable cord.
- You will need enough batting or bump interlining to fit the outside of the front and sides of the cornice box frame.

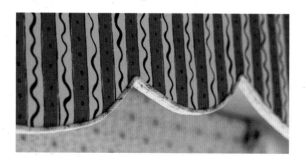

1 On paper, trace around the wooden cornice front and draw your chosen shape along the lower edge. Cut out the shape to form the front template. Trace the side-pieces and cut them out. Place the shaped template on the wooden front piece, 1½ inches from the bottom. Trace the lower shaped edge and cut it out with a jigsaw. On the shaped front piece, drill two holes along the side edges and six holes along the top, placing them ⅛ inch from the edge. Repeat on the top piece, drilling two holes along each end. Screw the front piece to the top piece along the top edge.

2 To complete the cornice box frame, screw the front piece to the front edges of the two side-pieces, and the top piece to the top edges of the two side-pieces, as shown.

TIP

Slipstitching makes an invisible edge, but for a quicker version, neatly staple the lining to the edges or disguise staples with braid trim.

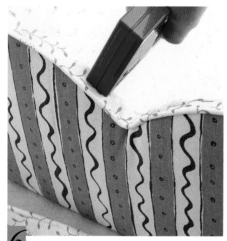

6 Make the cording from the contrast fabric, as shown on page 196. Staple the covered cording to the lower edges of the cornice, making sure that the cord faces outward and that the flanged edges lay along the lower edges of the cornice, as shown.

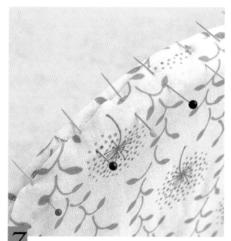

7 Remove the tape and use the front template to cut out the front contrast lining fabric, adding a ¾-inch hem allowance around all sides. Fold under a ⅜-inch hem along the lining lower edge, and pin the lining to the front cornice edges, butting the folded edge up to the covered cording. Snip into the corners as you work.

8 Smooth out the lining fabric along the inside of the front cornice box, pushing it well into the corners. Staple it in place at the sides and top. Using the curved upholstery needle, slipstitch the pinned lower edge of the lining to the cornice. (See page 190.)

3 Lay the front template flat and place a side-piece at each side edge, keeping them ⅜ inch apart. Using tape, temporarily attach the sides to the front. Use the taped templates to cut out the batting. Attach the batting to the front and sides of the cornice box with adhesive.

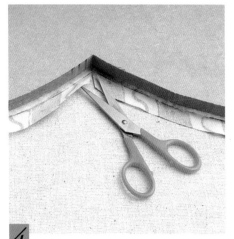

4 Using the taped templates, cut out the main fabric adding a ⅝-inch hem allowance all around. Lay the main fabric piece down on a flat surface, with the wrong side up. Place the covered front of the cornice box in the center, on top, with ⅝ inch of the fabric showing all around. Snip into any fabric curves along the bottom edge.

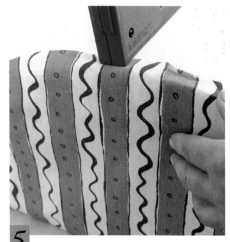

5 Using the staple gun, carefully fasten the fabric to the cornice box, placing the staples along the edges of the board and slightly stretching the fabric as you work, as shown here. Fold the fabric at the corners to get it around the side edges.

9 Using the template, cut out two side-pieces from the contrast fabric, adding a ¾-inch hem allowance all around. Pin and slipstitch the side linings to the lower corded edge, as shown for the front piece. Then fold under and staple the fabric along the side back edges and the front and top inside edges. Fix the cornice above your window treatment using the angle iron. (See page 189.)

VARIATION

If you love the idea of a scalloped pelmet, but want something a little less structured, try this simple idea. Put up a mounting board and cut shaped, curved fabric pieces that will overlap to fit along the board. Stitch small hems to the curved edge of each one and staple them in place to the top of the mounting board. Overlap the fabric to form a scalloped edge along the bottom.

Fold-Over Panel

Found in a country market in France, this antique linen tea towel seemed too good for drying the dishes, so now it's been turned into a simple panel for a kitchen window. Thrown over a slim metal rod, the light filters through the creamy texture of the linen, showing off the hand-woven stripes to perfection. This panel is short and skims the top of the flowers on the windowsill, but if you wanted yours to be longer, pin cotton tapes to the top edge, and tie them to the rod.

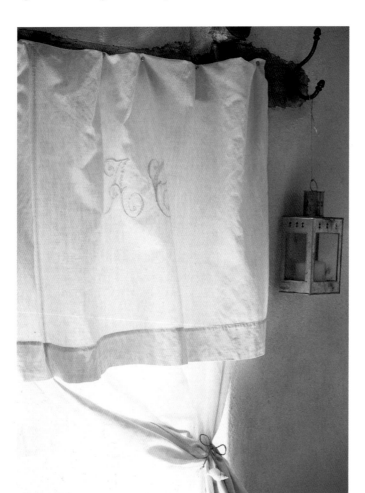

VARIATION

A beautiful, antique French linen sheet was too precious to cut up, so it has been pinned along an ancient beam. The hand-sewn monogram falls over to the front and the sheet is tied back across the window with a length of jute string for a rustic look.

Fabric Tiebacks

Tiebacks are not only attractive, but they are very useful, especially with full-length draperies at doors or windows where space is restricted. They keep the panels fixed and out of the way. Crescent-shaped tiebacks can be made from matching drapery fabric or from a contrasting fabric to coordinate with your room.

YOU WILL NEED

- Main decorator fabric, to match or contrast your drapes—see right for estimating the yardage

- Drapery lining—see right for estimating the yardage

- Stiff cornice stiffener or non-fusible interfacing—see right for estimating the yardage

- Two brass or plastic curtain rings for each tieback

- Paper and pencil for making a paper pattern. (See page 200.)

ESTIMATING THE FABRIC

- Once you have made your paper pattern, allow for one piece of main fabric, plus a ⅝-inch seam allowance all around, per tieback.

- For the lining you will need the same quantity as the main fabric.

- For the stiffener or interfacing allow for one piece, with no extra allowances, per tieback.

PREPARATION

- Cut out all the pieces for each tieback, drawing around the pattern piece and remembering to add an extra ⅝-inch seam allowance around the sides on the main fabric and lining.

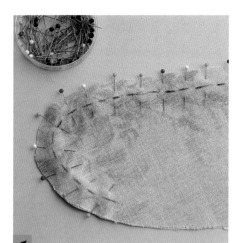

1 With right sides facing, lay the main fabric and lining together and pin around the side, top, and curved edges, leaving the lower edge open. Machine-stitch together with a ⅝-inch seam allowance.

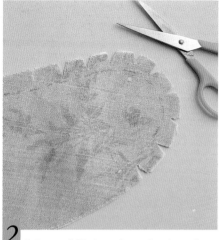

2 Snip small V-shaped notches into the curved seam allowances around the stitched upper edges.

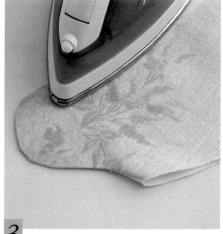

3 Turn the tieback through to the right side. Carefully tease out the seamed edges into smooth curves, before pressing them flat.

5 Make a ⅜-inch snip into the seam allowances at the outer corners of the lower opening.

6 Press both the opening edges ⅝ inch onto the wrong side along the curved lower edge, folding them up to the lining side of the tieback.

7 Pin and baste the lower pressed edges together. Slipstitch the lower edges together. (See page 190.) Then remove the basting stitches.

4 Insert the stiffener into the open edges of the tieback. Smooth the seam allowances down along the lining side of the stiffener. Trim the stiffener, if necessary, until it fits snugly.

8 With the lining side of the tieback facing up, oversew a curtain ring to each curved end of the tieback by hand. (See page 190.) Allow the ring to slightly overhang the edge. Slip one of the rings over a tieback hook attached to the side of the window, then loop the tieback around the drape and slip the second ring over the same hook.

TIP

This type of fabric tieback looks great if it is decorated with fabric-covered cording around the edge. (See page 196.) To do this, baste and machine-stitch, using a zipper foot on your machine, the cording around the edges of the main fabric piece, in step 1, before attaching the lining. Continue as before. Alternatively, hand-stitch a decorative drapery cord around the edges after the tieback is complete.

VARIATION

Tiebacks come in many different guises, and can make all the difference if you want to give a room a slightly formal or traditional look. Allow the curtain to slightly billow out above the tieback, which can be a formal, tasseled style, or just a simple wooden boss to hold lined draperies back from the window.

Soft Sash Tieback

Perfect for a child's bedroom, these simple sash tiebacks are ideal for holding back lightweight cotton curtains on a window. In a fresh blue stripe and plain lime green, these bias-edged tiebacks are an alternative to formal styles, and are easy for children to tie.

YOU WILL NEED

- Main decorator fabric—see right for estimating the yardage

- Contrast decorator fabric—see right for estimating the yardage

- Contrast decorator fabric for the bias edging—see right for estimating the yardage

- Matching sewing thread

- One brass or plastic curtain ring

- Paper for making a paper pattern

- A fabric or plastic measuring tape

- A drinking cup

ESTIMATING YARDAGE

- Determine the length of your tieback. To do this, wrap your measuring tape around your curtain, and loosely tie the ends together, allow about 8 inches beyond the knot for tails at each end. Unwrap the measuring tape and make a note of the length.

- Draw a long pattern piece on the paper, 3¾-inches wide, by the length calculated. Curve the ends of the strip by tracing around the top curved edge of an up-turned drinking cup. Cut out the pattern piece. For each tieback, you will need to allow for one tieback strip from main fabric and one from contrast fabric.

- For the bias-edging, measure around the total outer edge of the tieback strip. Allow for enough 1½-inch-wide bias-grain strips of the second contrast fabric to fit around the measured outer edge of the tieback, plus ⅝ inch for joining. (See page 200.)

TIP

For speed, buy ready-made 1-inch-wide bias binding, instead of cutting out and making up your own from contrast fabric.

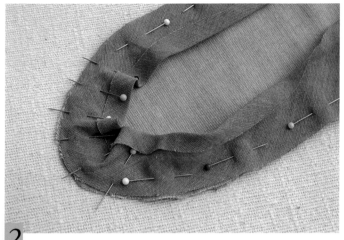

1 For each tieback, cut out one tieback strip from main fabric, one from contrast, and the bias-grain strips from the second contrast fabric. With right sides together, join the bias-grain strips to obtain your correct length, and press the long raw edges over to the wrong side to meet down the center to form bias binding. (See page 200.) With right sides facing, lay the main fabric strip over the contrast fabric strip and baste them together around the edges.

2 Open one long-pressed edge of the bias binding, and with right sides together and raw edges matching, place the edge along the basted edges of the tieback strip. Pin the bias binding in place all around the edge, using the press line as a guide and placing the pins at right angles around the curved ends to help ease the fabric around the shape. Neatly finish the binding ends. Turn under ⅜ inch at one end of the binding and slip the folded end under the raw end. Pin in place.

3 Machine-stitch the bias binding in place, stitching along the press line. Remove the basting stitches.

4 Fold up the bias binding back along the pressed and stitched line. Then take the opposite long pressed edge and bring it over onto the other side of the tieback, lining it up with the row of machine stitching. Pin it in place and slipstitch the pressed edge to the machine stitches. (See page 190.) Remove the pins.

5 Hand catchstitch the curtain ring to the center of the tieback on the right side along the bias edging. (See page 191.)

Make an easy tieback for an organza curtain by stringing glass beads along a length of nylon thread. Vary the sizes and shapes of the beads and use a double length of thread. Attach a curtain ring to both ends of the thread. Use these to hang the curtain to hang over a small hook fixed to the wall behind the curtain.

Basic Techniques

Here are all the basic techniques you need to make the projects in this book, from measuring windows to caring for fabrics, as well as all the stitches and sewing techniques.

Choosing Fabrics

Having chosen your style of window treatment, you need to decide what material you will use to make it. Fabric choice is a matter of taste, but with so many drapery fabrics on the market today, it is difficult to know where to start. There are heavy linens, textured weaves, silks, thick velvets, fine sheers, and many more. Once you have decided on the type of fabric, you must choose a color or print. The color may be determined by the decor of your room. But do you want a traditional floral, a glazed chintz, a geometric pattern, or stripes? The real starting point for choosing any fabric is to make sure it is right for the job. Take several small samples home with you, and when you have decided on your favorite, either borrow a large sample from the shop, or invest in a yard.

Look at it in both natural and artificial light, and think about the size of any pattern repeats. The color will look darker in a large sample and patterns can look totally different when viewed from a distance. Hang the sample in the window, drape and fold it to see how it reacts.

Finally, don't skimp on the fabric yardage; full draperies made from inexpensive fabrics look much better than ones that have been made from half the amount of a high-price fabric.

Cotton is a good choice because it is hard-wearing and inexpensive, and it drapes well. It is usually washable, too.

However, cotton can shrink, so be sure to buy a pre-shrunk variety, or launder it before you make the curtains.

If you want a soft, billowing look, choose a silk taffeta, or synthetic equivalent. Silks, satins, taffetas, and the various synthetic varieties possess excellent draping qualities and are available in a wide range of colors and patterns. Natural silk is expensive, and can rot over time if it is exposed to strong natural sunlight, unless it is properly lined. A lookalike is often a much better choice.

Linen and a cotton and linen blend are the most hard-wearing fabrics available. As a rule, the more expensive the linen, the softer the fabric and the better it will drape.

Cutting Out

You will need a large flat surface and a sharp pair of scissors. Before you start to cut out, check the entire length of the fabric for faults and double-check all your calculations to make sure that you have added in the correct hem allowances and pattern repeats. Iron out any creases.

Form a straight line across the fabric at right angles to the selvage. With loosely woven fabrics, you can do this by pulling a crosswise thread from the weave of the fabric. For other fabric types, you will need to use a triangle, dressmakers' chalk, and a long straightedge, to mark and cut the fabric straight across, at right angles to the selvage. Measure each fabric length and mark the cutting point with pin, then check that it is correct. Always double-check all your measurements before cutting the fabric.

If you are using a fabric that has a pattern repeat, place an entire pattern repeat at the lower edge, rather than the top. Mark the top of each cut length of fabric with dressmakers' chalk, to make sure that

MATCHING PATTERN REPEATS

It is important to make sure that the leading edges of all pairs of drapes and curtains match exactly, and that the design lines up correctly across any seams. The best way is to match the pattern repeats before sewing.

1 Lay one of the cut lengths of fabric on a flat surface, right side up. On another length of fabric, fold over the seam allowance along one side edge and press lightly.

2 With right sides uppermost, overlap the pressed edge over the side edge of the first fabric length, matching up the pattern along the edges. Pin the pieces together and then baste them with ladder stitch. Remove all pins and open out the seam allowances and machine-stitch together as usual from the wrong side.

3 Remove the basting stitches. If the background of the fabric is a dark color, or the selvages are tightly woven, press the seam allowances open and snip into the selvages at 2-inch intervals. If the background color is pale, trim the selvages back to ⅝ inch, removing any printed words along the edges.

you stitch the lengths together all facing the same direction. This is especially important when you are working with fabrics that have a nap.

Try not to fold cut lengths of fabric, but if you must, fold them lengthwise, so that any creases that form will be hidden in the finished folds of the curtains.

Tracks and Poles

All curtains need to be suspended in front of the window in some way, and there are several ways to do it. Unless you plan to use a cornice or valance, which will cover the system or utilitarian rod, use a wooden or metal pole that can stand on its own right decoratively speaking. The decorative finials at each end can be sculptural or ornate, such as acanthus leaf and pineapple finials, or much simpler, round knobs, for example.

Cast-iron poles are very popular, too, and these can have equally decorative scrolled or curled ends. Use antiqued wooden poles or black cast-iron in a Scandinavian-style room, natural wood with a country decor, and brushed steel in a more contemporary setting.

Slip matching wooden or metal rings onto the poles, which can be suspended by brackets on either side of the window. A very long pole may need a center bracket for additional support. Curtain panels can be attached to rods or poles with hooks that are inserted into either the heading tape or the eyelets of the rings.

Some of the latest solutions are simple and high-tech: fine, high-tension wires fit through eyelets; cleverly designed clips hold fabric securely in place without sewing; and small metal clips with teeth that suspend a swathe of fabric from a pole. Be sure that they won't rip a delicate sheer fabric.

There is a wide range of poles and finials available, from contemporary brushed steel poles to carved and gilded finials, like the ones shown here.

Caring for Drapes and Shades

Regular care and attention will prevent window treatments from becoming too dirty.

Vacuuming

The regular removal of dust will prevent household dirt from settling deep down into the fibers of your curtains and shades. Once the dirt has penetrated, it is often difficult to remove. Vacuum all window treatments with a soft brush attachment, paying attention to the inside of pleats and ruffles.

Airing

One of the simplest ways to freshen up draperies and curtains is to throw the windows wide open on a fine, dry, breezy day, then draw the panels closed and let them blow freely for a few hours. This will help to remove any stale household smells or dust mites. If it's possible, hang them on an outdoor clothesline for an afternoon.

Laundering

Unlined drapes may be washed if you wish, but the fabric may lose any special finishes, which could affect the curtains' body. If there is a care label attached to the roll of fabric when you buy it, save it for your reference. Also, do a test: cut an 8-inch square of the fabric and wash it. After it's dry and you've ironed it, measure the sample to see if it has shrunk. If it has, either hand-wash the curtains in cold water or have them professionally cleaned.

Iron the curtain while it is still damp, carefully pressing over seams so the ridges do not make marks to show through. Set the iron on a cool temperature and use a pressing cloth to prevent shine and scorching. If you have a steamer, use it to take out any other wrinkles once the curtain is hung.

Dry cleaning

This is really the only option for lined draperies and shades. However, dry cleaning should be avoided, if possible, in favor of regular airing and vacuuming.

Hardware maintenance

To keep your curtain hardware in good working order, treat the inside of traverse rods and the top of poles with an anti-static spray from time to time. Use a soft brush to keep finials and curtain rings dust-free, too.

How to Measure for Curtains and Draperies

When measuring for curtains and draperies, it may be helpful if the hardware (rods and traverse rods) is in place before you begin, including carpets for full-length curtains and drapes.

Always use a long, retractable steel measuring tape, and ask someone to help you when measuring large windows. Decide on the type of heading you will be making, because it can affect the location of the rod in relation to the top of the window or the trim.

Curtain width or fullness

The fabric fullness required will depend on the curtain heading (see the individual projects). Generally, for each panel, allow one-and-a-half to two-and-a-half times the width of the rod, divided by two.

Curtain length or drop

For the finished length (drop) of the curtains, measure as follows:

- For curtains hung from an exposed traverse rod, work out where the heading will finish in relation to the track. If you are unsure, use drapery hooks to attach a piece of heading pleater tape to the track, and measure down from the top of the tape.
- For curtains hung from a rod, measure the length from the bottom of the curtain ring or the eyelet.
- For curtains hung from a traverse rod that is attached to a cornice mounting board, measure the finished length (drop) from the underside of the board, then deduct the hook drop. This will depend on the type of heading and hardware you are using. If you are unsure, hook a piece of the chosen pleater tape to the track with drapery hooks. Measure the clearance between the top edge of the tape and the bottom edge of the board.

- For full-length curtains, deduct ⅜ inch from measurement B (see diagram below left), for clearance. If you prefer to pool curtains on the floor, add another 6 to 8 inches to measurement B.
- For sill-length curtains, add 2 to 4 inches to measurement C so that they hang just below the windowsill. If the sill protrudes, deduct ⅜ inch from measurement C (see diagram), to allow the curtains to hang clear.

MEASURING FOR CURTAINS

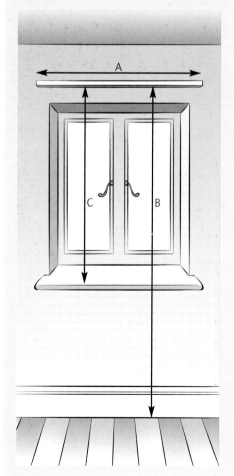

There are two main measurements needed for working out the fabric yardage: the length of the rod, the traverse rod (including any overlap arms at the center, if your rod has them), or the cornice mounting board (measurement A on the diagram, left), and the length (or drop) from the drapery hardware to the floor (measurement B on the diagram) or windowsill (measurement C on the diagram), depending on the style of your draperies.

Measure the finished length (drop) a few times across the window, as floors can be uneven. Check whether the window is plumb (an even square or rectangle), by measuring the width at both the top and bottom. Check every measurement twice.

Estimating yardage

First, calculate how many fabric widths are needed. Take your finished curtain-width (fullness) measurement and divide it by the width of your fabric.

For example: for a finished curtain width of 90 inches and a fabric width of 54 inches, you will need two widths per curtain. If the number of fabric widths works out to be just under or over a number of full widths, round up or down to the nearest full width. If it is nearer a half width, round it up or down to the nearest half width, and place the half panels on the outer edges of the curtains when stitching them together.

Next, calculate the total yardage. Add the top and lower hem allowances to the length (drop) measurements (see the individual projects) and multiply this number by the quantity of fabric widths calculated.

If your fabric has a pattern repeat, add one full pattern repeat per width of fabric, after the first width.

How to Measure for Shades

A shade requires a mounting board for installation. As with curtains and draperies, it is helpful to have the board in place before you measure (see Making a Mounting Board, on page 188). Shades can either be installed inside the window recess or frame, or outside, on or above the top trim. Inside mounts look neater with Swedish and Roman shades, but they may block out some daylight or obstruct some windows from opening. Outside mounts allow more flexibility if you need to disguise the shape of a window, and they also admit more light.

Dowel-rod spacing for Roman shades

Measure your window, as illustrated above right, to find the finished width and length of your shade.

For an average shade, allow 4 inches between the position of the lowest dowel-rod casing and the hem edge (half a pleat depth), unless otherwise specified (see the diagram below right). Place the top dowel-rod casing 12 inches from the top edge of the shade (one and a half times the pleat depth). Space the remaining dowel-rod casings evenly, approximately 8 inches apart (a full pleat depth), depending on the size of your window.

For a lined Roman shade, add 1¼ inches to the finished length of the shade per dowel-rod casing, plus the hem allowances.

Estimating yardage for shades

To calculate yardage, use the length of the mounting board for the width measurement and multiply by the length or drop of the shade. Remember, these are your finished shade measurements only—turn to the individual projects to find out the hem and seam allowances required.

MEASURING FOR SHADES

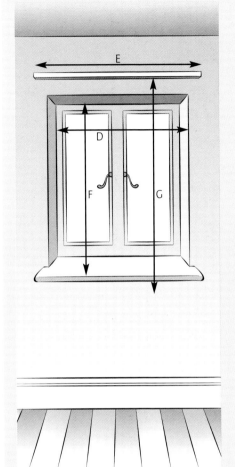

For an inside mount, screw the mounting board directly to the top of the window recess or into the top of the frame. The mounting board should be the width of the window recess or the width inside the casing from left to right (measurement D on the diagram, left), minus ⅜ inch each side, so the shade will not touch the sides of the window, which could restrict it from moving up and down correctly.

For an outside mount, the mounting board should be the width of the window plus 4–6 inches on either side. Screw it either directly into the wall above the window (see measurement E) or onto the top trim.

Shade length or drop

To work out the finished length or drop of an inside-mount, measure from the top of the mounting board to the sill, minus ⅜ inch, (measurement F).

For the finished length or drop of an outside-mount shade, measure from the top of the mounting board to a point that is 2 inches below the sill (measurement G).

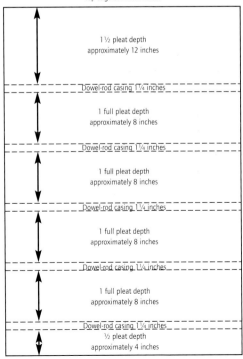

Top edge of Roman shade

1½ pleat depth
approximately 12 inches

Dowel-rod casing 1¼ inches

1 full pleat depth
approximately 8 inches

Dowel-rod casing 1¼ inches

1 full pleat depth
approximately 8 inches

Dowel-rod casing 1¼ inches

1 full pleat depth
approximately 8 inches

Dowel-rod casing 1¼ inches

1 full pleat depth
approximately 8 inches

Dowel-rod casing 1¼ inches

½ pleat depth
approximately 4 inches

MAKING A MOUNTING BOARD

The mounting board for a shade is used to attach the shade to the window frame or the surrounding wall. It is made from a piece of 1 x 2-inch wood, which is usually covered in fabric to match your shade.

MAKING A WOODEN LATH

Cut a mounting board to the finished width of the shade (see "Fixing Shades," on page 187). For an inside mount, drill a hole at each end of the underside of the board, 6 inches from the edge. For an outside mount, drill a hole into the face of the board, at each end, 6 inches from the edge.

1 For both inside- and outside-mount shades, cut a strip of fabric wide enough to wrap around the board and hang about 4 inches longer than the board. Place the board in the center on the wrong side of the fabric strip, and fold the fabric ends up and onto the top. Staple in place.

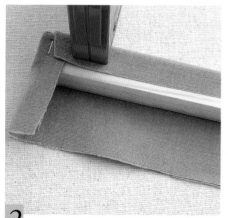

2 Fold the ends of the fabric into envelope corners, wrap the sides of the fabric around the board and staple in place along the entire length.

3 Staple the hook side of the hook-and-loop tape to the top of the covered board for an outside-mount shade. This will hide the stitching at the top of the shade from view, but remember to allow for the extra length (depth of the board) at the top of the shade when estimating yardage. For an inside-mount shade, staple the hook side of hook-and-loop tape to the front of the board.

4 Using a bradawl, mark the positions of the screw eyes on the underside of the lath. Line them up with the rows of cording rings on the shade and screw them in place. Attach an extra eye 1 inch from one end of the mounting board, on the cord-operating side.

MAKING AND INSTALLING A CORNICE MOUNTING BOARD

A mounting board for a cornice must be made from sturdy wood that does not bend, such as pine or plywood that is about 1 inch thick.

1 Make the board 5–8 inches deep, depending on your project, so that it projects far enough beyond the traverse rod to allow draperies to move freely behind it. The length of the board should be the same length as the traverse rod, plus 1 inch at each end.

2 Cover the board with fabric that you can attach to the underside with staples. Alternatively, paint the board to match your decor.

3 Staple the hook side of a length of hook-and-loop tape to the narrow front and side edges of the board, for attaching the cornice later.

4 Using angle irons, attach the mounting board to the wall above the window, just above the trim. Mount the traverse rod to the underside of the board halfway in from the edge, so that the draperies can be drawn easily when the cornice is in place.

INSTALLING A SHADE'S MOUNTING BOARD

For an inside-mount shade, pierce the fabric covering the drilled holes and screw the board to the top of the window frame.

For an outside-mount shade, pierce the fabric covering the holes and screw the board directly into the wall or onto the trim above the window. Alternatively, screw small angle irons to the underside of the board, then secure the angle irons to the wall above the window.

If your mounting board will not be visible from the front, just cover the ends with fabric, or paint the board the same color as the wall or the window frame, depending on where it will be attached.

An easy way to fix a shade in place is to attach the shade to the mounting board with the hook-and-loop tape before the board is fixed in place. String the cord through all the rings, tape, and screw eyes, as instructed in the project. To fix the board, open the hook-and-loop tape to beyond the drilled holes. Fix the board in place and rejoin the hook-and-loop tape.

STITCHES

This is a selection of the stitches most commonly used in this book. In all cases, it is important to make the stitches an even size and keep an even tension. Work all stitches with a thread that matches the fabric. However, you can use a contrasting color to make temporary stitches easier to see when it's time to remove them. (A contrast-colored thread has been used for all stitches in these photographs, to make them easier to follow.)

The following stitches have been made by a right-handed person; simply reverse them if you are left-handed.

BASTING STITCH

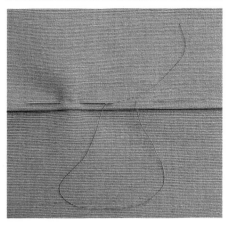

This is a temporary stitch used to hold two pieces of fabric together while the permanent stitching is being done. Using a contrasting-color thread, work long, straight stitches just inside the seam line by moving the needle in and out of the fabric.

LADDER STITCH

This is a temporary stitch worked from the right side of the fabric to hold two pieces of fabric together when matching patterns along a seam. It is worked like slip hemming, holding a folded edge to a flat surface.

Press the seam allowance over and along one long edge of the first piece of fabric. Then position it on the seam allowance of the second piece of fabric so the pattern matches. Pin together. Secure the thread inside the folded edge. Bring the needle out of the fold, insert it across the join and down through the flat fabric close to the seam. Insert the needle vertically along the underside of the seam for ¾ inch, then bring it out close to the seam. Make a horizontal stitch across the join into the folded edge, run the needle along the fold for ¾ inch, then bring it out and pull the thread through. Continue until the seam is basted. Remove the pins. The two pieces can now be folded right sides together for stitching.

EVEN SLIPSTITCH

This is an invisible stitch that is used to join two folded edges together, as in the case of attaching lining to the main fabric or closing the edges of a mitered corner.

Working from right to left, secure thread on the wrong side, then slip the needle through one of the folded edges, then through the opposite folded edge for about ¼ inch. Continue working in this way across the gap, closing the two edges together.

OVERHAND STITCH

A tiny even stitch, used to top-sew two finished or folded edges together, as in attaching ties, rings, or tapes.

Secure the thread on the wrong side of the fabric. Push the needle through to the front, close to the working edge. Bring it over the top of the edge, diagonally and to the left. Pick up one or two threads, then bring the needle back and through the front edge, picking up one or two threads from that side of the fabric, as before. Continue in this way, keeping the stitches uniform in size and evenly spaced.

SLIPSTITCH

This stitch is used to hold a folded hem edge to a flat surface. It is almost invisible on the right side of the fabric and is worked from the right to the left, holding the needle parallel to the stitching line.

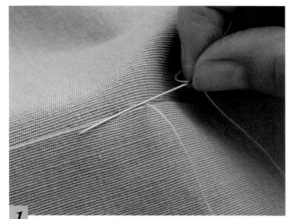

1 Secure the thread on the inside of the hem. Bring the needle out of the top fold of the hem and pick up two threads from the flat fabric directly below.

2 Insert the needle back down into the folded edge and run the needle inside the fold for approximately ⅜ inch. Bring the needle and thread back out. Continue along the hem in the same way, making sure the stitches are not pulled too tightly or the fabric will look puckered on the right side.

CATCHSTITCH

Used to hold a raw edge firmly against a flat surface. This stitch is worked from right to left, as in single-fold side hems that will be enclosed with a lining.

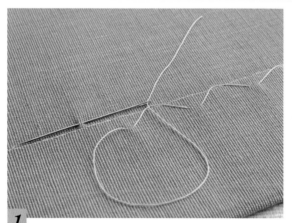

1 Secure the thread on the wrong side of the hem, bring the needle and thread through to the right side about ⅛ inch in from the raw edge. Pass the needle up and to the left, picking up two threads from the single layer of fabric.

2 Pull the needle and thread through and pass it down to the left, taking another tiny stitch in the hem fabric. Continue along the hem in this way.

SEAMS

There are several different types of seams used in this book. The right choice takes into account the weight and thickness of the fabric, and the position of the seam. Always make sure that you allow enough fabric for your seam allowances (turnings), especially if the fabric is likely to fray. In that case, neaten the edges with a machine zigzag stitch, a special serging machine, or by hand with an overhand stitch.

PLAIN SEAM

This is the most commonly used seam used for joining drapery fabric widths. It is best to use a ¾-inch-wide seam allowance when making curtains and draperies, unless otherwise stated.

1 With right sides together, machine-stitch along the seam line, making a few reverse stitches at the start and finish of the seam to secure the threads. If you prefer, pin and baste first.

2 Using a steam iron, press open the seam allowances against the wrong side of the fabric.

FRENCH SEAM

This narrow double seam neatly contains all the raw edges. It is used mainly on unlined items, sheer and lightweight fabrics, and those that fray easily.

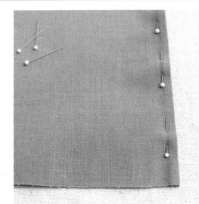

1 With wrong sides together, pin the two edges together and machine-stitch a line ⅜ inch in from the raw edge. Trim the seam allowances to ¼-inch wide and press them open.

2 Press the seam back onto itself so that right sides are together, with the seam-line running along the edge. Pin and machine-stitch the seam ⅜-inch from the folded edge, enclosing the raw edges. Press the finished seam to one side.

LAPPED SEAM

Interlinings are made from bulky fabrics and are best joined with a lapped seam, which gives a completely flat finish. Because the seams will be enclosed within the item, there is no need to neaten the edges.

With both pieces of interlining right side up, overlap one raw edge directly over the other by ½–¾ inch.

Pin and machine-stitch the two layers together using either straight or zigzag stitch. Trim the raw edges.

FLAT FELL SEAM

This is another type of self-neatening seam, used mainly for heavier weight fabrics, where the raw edges are enclosed. It is stronger and flatter than a French seam.

1 With right sides together, pin the two joining edges and machine-stitch along the seam line, making a few reverse stitches at the start and finish of the seam to secure the threads. Press open the seam allowances and trim one of them to ¼-inch wide.

2 Fold the other seam allowance in half and over to the raw edge of the trimmed seam allowance. Press the seam flat.

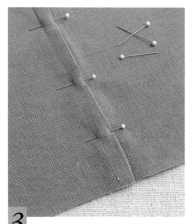

3 Pin the seam allowances at right angles to the seam and machine-stitch them in place close to the folded edge.

REDUCING BULK

Before turning out a seamed corner, trim away the seam allowances, so that they are less bulky and sit flat when pressed.

1 Snip the seam allowances at the corner close to the stitched line, as shown. Be careful not to cut too close, otherwise frayed edges will pop out on the right side.

2 If the seam is still bulky because the fabric is thick, snip away more from the seam allowance on each side of the corner in a diagonal line, as shown.

3 Use a pointed object, such as a pair of scissors, to carefully push out the corner on the right side. Be careful not to push through the seam.

Hems

In order to create a flat hem, you must make sure that fabric lengths are cut straight. As long as you have a straight edge, it is simple to fold over the required amount and press it in place with a steam iron. Most base hems are made with a double-fold, although a lot of side hems may be just a single-fold, especially if they are enclosed within the lining. If you want hems to be invisible from the right side of your draperies, hem them (see page 191) in place by hand with a slipstitch. Alternatively, on more informal curtains and panels, you can machine-stitch hems in place.

(see page 191)

WEIGHTS

It is advisable to insert weights into the hems of draperies and curtains, especially if they are full-length panels. Weights help the fabric to hang better by holding it down and keeping the hems straight and even. Weights are sewn into the mitered corners of each hem and at each fabric width or half width across the hem.

1 Cut two square pieces of lining about ¾ inch larger than the diameter of the weight. Pin the pieces together along three sides.

TIPS

- You can buy round or rectangular lead weights. The round ones often have two holes drilled into the center, rather like a button, so you can sew them directly onto the fabric. For a neater finish, make small lining pockets to encase the weights. Then slipstitch the pockets into the base hem.

- You can also buy lead-weight tape. This is a length of chain that is sold by the yard. It is particularly good for lightweight and sheer fabrics. The weighted tape is threaded into the entire hem and secured in place at regular intervals with a hand stitch.

2 Machine-stitch the pockets around the three-pinned sides. Insert a weight and machine-stitch across the fourth side to close the pocket.

MITERING CORNERS

A miter is used to form a neat, flat finish at a corner where two hems meet.

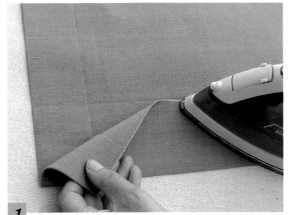

1 Press the required hem allowances onto the sides and along the bottom edges.

2 Open the hems flat again. Matching up the press lines, turn over the corner of the fabric so that the diagonal fold passes through the point where the two inner press lines cross. Press the diagonal fold flat.

3 Refold the side hem back in place again and slip a covered weight (see previous page) under the edge of the side hem. Pin and hand-stitch it in place. Turn the first fold of the base hem back over to the wrong side.

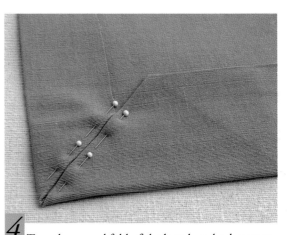

4 Turn the second fold of the base hem back over to the wrong side, enclosing the covered weight. Pin the diagonal mitered edges in place. The hem is now ready to be stitched in place.

CORDING AND PIPING

Cording is a soft cord that is covered with a narrow strip of fabric. It is sewn into a seam as a decorative edging to make the seam stronger. If your cord is not pre-shrunk, wash and dry it at a high temperature. Cable cord is available in various diameters, although the medium sizes, 3 and 4, are most commonly used.

CUTTING AND JOINING CORDING STRIPS

If the cording is to be used in a straight line, cut the fabric strips along the straight grain. You may also do this if you are using a striped fabric and want the stripes to run in a horizontal direction around the cord. However, if the cording will curve around corners, cut the strips on the bias (at a 45-degree angle to the horizontal and cross grains) to help them bend. This means cutting them at an angle to the warp and weft threads of the fabrics.

1 To find the bias of the fabric, fold down the raw edge that is running across the width of the fabric from selvage to selvage to form a triangle that lies parallel to one of the selvages. Press and cut along the fold line.

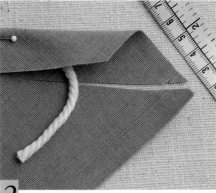

2 Draw the required width in chalk lines parallel to the bias cut line. To gauge the strip width, measure around the cord and add the correct seam allowance. (See the individual project.) Alternatively, fold a corner of the fabric over the cord and pin, encasing the cord snugly; then measure the seam allowance from the pin and cut.

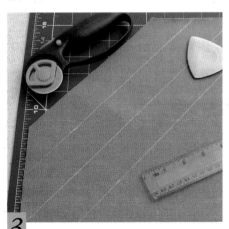

3 Open the fabric strip to find the correct cutting width. Cut along the lines using scissors or a rotary cutter, ruler, and mat, until you have the required number of strips to go around the edge of your project.

4 To join the fabric cording strips to form one length, trim the ends at a 45-degree angle. With right sides facing, stitch the two pieces together with a ¼ inch seam allowance.

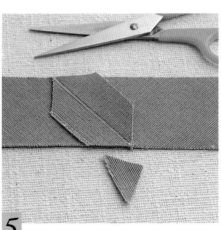

5 Press open the seam and trim the pointed ends of the seam allowances level with the edges of the strip.

JOINING CORDING ENDS

You will have to join cord ends to make one continuous seam.

Note: So that you can see how the ends are joined, in these photos (right) the length of cording is not basted to a fabric piece.

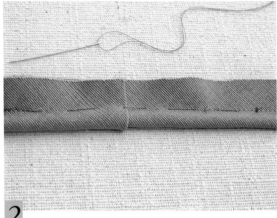

1 Once you have basted your cording to the right side of the fabric piece, pick out about 2 inches of the cording machine stitches at each end, where the ends meet, and fold back the cording fabric strips. Trim the two ends of the cord so that they butt together, then bind the ends with thread.

2 Turn under ⅜ inch at one end of the fabric strip to neaten, and slip this end over the raw end opposite. Baste the ends together, enclosing the cable cord inside, and continue as shown in the individual project.

COVERING CABLE CORD

1 Place the cable cord on the wrong side of the cording strip and bring the long edges together, enclosing the cord. Pin the edges together.

2 Using a zipper foot on your sewing machine, stitch down the length of the cord, working as close to the cable cord as possible.

CORDING RIGHT ANGLES AND CURVES

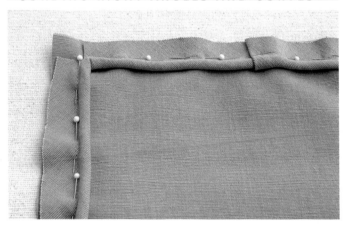

Pin and baste the cording to the right side of the one fabric piece, with raw edges level and the cord facing inward. To make the cording turn the corner, clip into the cording seam allowances close to the stitch line and bend the cord around the corner. Continue basting the cording in place, as before.

If the cording is to bend gradually around a curve, snip into the cording seam allowances at several regular intervals so that the cord curves around smoothly.

MAKING TIES

Narrow fabric ties can be used instead of more formal curtain headings. They are ideal for attaching a pair of simple curtains to a pole for an informal look, as shown in the projects featured on pages 26 and 36.

These narrow fabric ties are cut and folded like bias binding and topstitched down one edge.

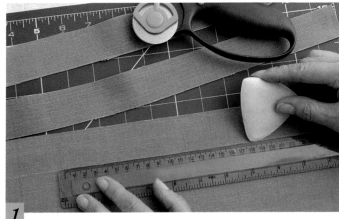

1 Draw parallel straight grain lines across the width your fabric, in the required tie width. This should be four times the finished flat width of the ties. Cut along the lines until you have the required length for your ties.

2 With wrong sides together, press the strip in half along the length. Then open the strip and press the long raw edges to the wrong side to meet the press line in the center, making sure you don't burn your fingers.

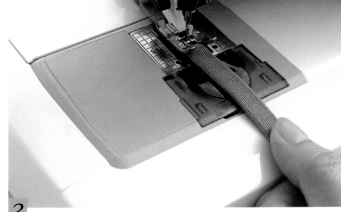

3 Fold the strip in half again along the length, bringing the pressed long edges together and enclosing the raw edges completely. Pin and machine-stitch the pressed edges along the full length of the strip. Cut the strip into the required lengths and number of ties. Neaten the raw ends by pushing them up inside the tie tubes.

MAKING TAB LOOPS

These tabs are made from strips of fabric that are stitched on the wrong side and turned out, so no topstitching or seams are visible on the finished side.

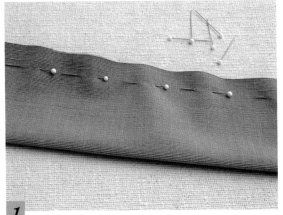

1 Cut out the tab strips to the size given in the individual project. With right sides together, fold a strip in half along its length. Pin and machine-stitch the long edges, with a ⅝-inch seam allowance, to form a tube.

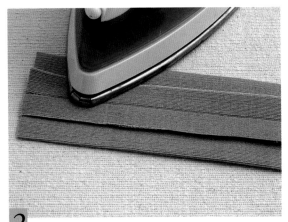

2 Fold the tube again so that the seam runs down the middle on one side, and press open the seam allowances.

3 Turn the tube through to the right side and press the tab flat making sure the seam is still running down the center of one side.

CALCULATING QUANTITIES OF TAB LOOPS AND TIES

To work out the number of tabs or loops needed for a project, take the finished width of your curtain panel and check the tab or loop spacing suggested for the individual project. Divide the finished curtain panel width by the spacing measurement. You will need one more loop than the number of spaces calculated.

For example: a curtain that is 60 inches wide with a tab spacing of 8 inches will have seven and a half spaces. Round down the figure to make seven full spaces and you will need eight tabs. If you round up the figure to eight spaces, you will need nine tabs. Whether you round the figure up or down will depend on how close you want the tabs or ties to sit along the heading.

BIAS BINDING

Bias binding is a strip of fabric cut on the cross, meaning cut at an angle to the warp and weft threads. If pressed in half along its length, bias binding can be used as a decorative edging—for example, neatened tieback edges. Follow step one of "Cutting and joining cording strips," on page 196, to find the bias of the fabric. Draw chalk lines parallel to the bias, in the required width (usually four times the finished width of your binding). Cut out the required number of strips to form the length necessary to go around the edge of the project.

PINCH PLEATS

Pinch pleats are a deep formal heading in which the flat drape is punctuated at regular intervals by pleats in groups of two or three. (See page 50.)

TIEBACKS

Tiebacks are a useful method of holding bulky drapes clear of the window, to let in as much light as possible. To calculate the finished length, hold a measuring tape around the drape to take in as much fullness as required. Allow about 1 inch for attaching the rings and hooks to hold the tiebacks.

CUTTING AND MAKING BIAS BINDING

1 Follow steps 4 and 5 of "Joining the cording strips," on page 196, for the finished length. With wrong sides together, fold the strip along its length, matching the long edges, and press.

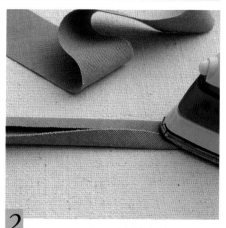

2 Open the strip and fold the long raw edges over to meet down the center press line on the wrong side of the fabric. Press the edges in place, taking care not to burn your fingers.

CALCULATING SPACES FOR PINCH-PLEAT HEADING

• Lay out flat the made-up panel and measure the width. Subtract from this the width of the finished (gathered up) drape. The difference between the two is the amount left over for the pleats. At each edge, there should be a flat allowance of 3¼ inches for rod overlap arms and returns.

• As a rough guide, allow four pleats for every width of fabric. Divide the amount leftover for the pleats by the total number of pleats calculated, to work out the size of the individual pleats.

• On the finished heading, excluding the overlap and return allowances at each side, you will have one less space than pleat. For example, if a panel is two fabric widths wide, it will have eight pleats and nine spaces. The two outer spaces at each end will be for the overlap and return allowances, which each measure 3¼ inches wide.

• To calculate the size of the spaces, subtract the overlap and return allowances (6½ inches in total) from the finished width of the curtain, and divide the remaining width by the number of spaces (7 in this example).

MAKING A SHAPED TEMPLATE

• Tiebacks that curve upward from the center can look very graceful. The lower edge may be scalloped or edged for extra decoration.

• The depth of the center section is a matter of choice and can be between 3 and 8 inches, curving up with pointed, flat, or rounded ends. Practice drawing different shapes on paper and hold them against your curtains to judge the scale.

• To make the final pattern of your desired tieback shape, fold a piece of paper to half the measured tieback length. Placing the center of the tieback to the fold in the paper to make sure that both sides will be the same, draw and cut out the desired shape. Unfold the pattern and position it around your curtain to see if you are happy with the shape and size.

MAKING TEMPLATES

If you are making a curtain heading with a shaped top, or a shade or cornice with a shaped base, make a template before you begin. This is a good way of checking that the individual shapes are all the same size and that you are pleased with the overall design. Your template will act as a pattern from which to cut out your pieces without making any mistakes during the cutting process.

SCALLOPED EDGE

See the Scalloped Panel on page 102.

- On a piece of paper, draw a strip to the final cutting dimensions of the lower facing. Subtract the hem and seam allowances by reducing the length of the facing by 1½ inches and the depth by 1¼ inches—measurements as given for the Scalloped Panel, on page 102.

- Decide on the finished width of the scallops, between 3 and 4 inches. A drinking cup or glass makes a good template for drawing the individual scallops. Measure the diameter of the cup and divide the facing length by the diameter to find the total number of scallops. For example: a cup measurement of 3½ inches divided into a facing length (the finished curtain width) of 60 inches will equal about 17 scallops.

- Draw a line on the paper template that is parallel to the lower edge, placing it half the diameter (the radius) of the cup measurement up from the lower edge.

A scalloped edge usually starts and finishes with a half-scallop (or as close to a half as your measurements will allow). Mark the scallops along the drawn line, marking a half-scallop at each end and full scallops (the cup's diameter) in between. Adjust the size of the end scallops, if necessary, to fit your finished measurement.

- Using the cup as a template, draw around the curved edges to form the scallops, placing the cup on the lower edge and between the scallop marks. When you have finished, carefully cut out the template.

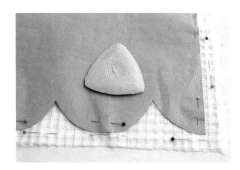

SCALLOPED HEADING

See the Café Curtains on page 76.

- On a piece of paper, draw a strip to the final cutting dimensions of the top facing. Subtract the hem and seam allowances by reducing the length of the facing by ¾ inches and the depth by ⅞ inches—measurements given for the Café Curtains, on page 76.

- The scallop size will depend on the width of the curtain, but as a general rule 4 inches is an average size for a scallop, with a 2½ inch strip in between. To work out the number of scallops, divide the finished curtain width by the sum of the scallop and a strip, in this case 6½ inches. There should be one more strip than scallop, with a strip section at each end.

- The shape of the scallops is based on a half-circle, so if you can find a drinking cup that is the right diameter this will help you to mark out you scallops. Otherwise, draw and cut out a circle that is the correct size from thin cardboard. Draw a line on the paper template that is parallel to the top edge, placing it 7 inches from the top edge. Mark the scallop and strip widths along the top edge of the facing, starting and finishing with a strip section at each end.

- Mark the same scallop and strip positions on the lower drawn line, then join the two pencil marks with vertical lines from the top edge of the facing to the lower line. Do this all along the entire length of the facing. Using the cup or cardboard circle, draw the scallop shapes by placing the edge of the cup or circle along the horizontal lower line and between two vertical scallop lines. Draw around the shape to form a curved lower edge. Repeat for all scallop shapes between each strip, then cut out the template.

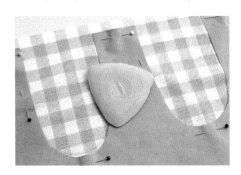

Resources

Fabrics used in the projects

Pages 22–25 Tie-Top Curtains
Antique French linen.

Pages 26–29 Simple Unlined Curtains
Antique French linen. Pole: Copes and
Timmins. Pillow fabric: Cabbages and
Roses.

Pages 30–35 Contrast-Lined Panels
Main fabric: Cockerel and Spot linen
union, Straw/Duck-egg/Raspberry, Vanessa
Arbuthnott; lining fabric: cotton ticking,
Peony, Ian Mankin. Variation: page 35,
Biggie Best.

Pages 36–39 Attic Window Curtain
Main fabric: Parterre linen union,
Cornflower/Cranberry; lining fabric: Polka
Dot Check linen union, Cranberry/Sea
pink, Vanessa Arbuthnott.

Pages 40–43 Appliquéd-Stripe Curtains
Main fabric: Seaweed and Shells linen
union, Forget-me-not; stripe fabric:
Deckchair Stripe linen union, Forget-me-
not/Denim, Vanessa Arbuthnott. Variation:
page 43, braid, V.V. Rouleaux.

Pages 44–49 Bordered Panels
Main fabric: Trellis, Blue; contrast fabric:
Tyrone, Wedgwood. Variation: page 49,
main fabric: Turquoise plain dye; contrast
fabric: Haven Stripe, Blue. All Elanbach.

Pages 52–55 Pinch-Pleat Draperies
Gulba 01, Malabar. Variation: page 55,
curtain, upholstery, pillow fabrics,
lampshade, all Kate Forman.

Pages 56–61 Pinch-Pleated Edged Panels
Main fabric: Out and About linen union,
Lettuce; contrast fabric: Dotty linen union,
Lettuce, Vanessa Arbuthnott. Variations:
page 60, Wilman; page 61, Laura Ashley.

Pages 62–67 Ruffle-Edged Curtains
Indian Organza, Gold Book, Malabar.

Pages 70–75 Two-Tone Panel
Main fabric: Bamboo, Chalk; contrast
fabric: Bamboo, Clay, Malabar.

Pages 76–79 Café Curtains
Gingham check, green, Jane Churchill.

Pages 80–83 Grommet-Top Panels
Woven ticking, Stone/Red, Cath Kidston.
Pole: Swish.

Pages 84–87 Shirred Rod-Pocket Curtains
Cameo Rose linen, Kate Forman; pom-
pom trim, V.V. Rouleaux. Variation:
page 97, Pret A Vivre.

Pages 88–91 Contrast-Top Tabbed Panels
French ready-made curtains. Variation:
page 91, Laura Ashley.

Pages 94–99 Cuffed Panels
Shot Cotton, Jade, Rowan. Variation:
page 99, Shot Cotton, Blush, Rowan;
beads, Ells & Farrier.

Pages 102–107 Scalloped Panel
Indian Muslin, Ivory Book, Malabar.
Variation: page 107, Luxaflex.

Pages 108–111 Ribbon-Tied Shade
Shanti, Rice, Malabar.

Pages 112–113 Cuff-Topped Muslins
Variation: page113, Walcot House.

Pages 114–117 Striped-Sheer Tabbed Panel
Akuti, 05, Malabar. Variation: page 117,
ready-made sheer panel, Breeze.

Pages 118–119 Swag-Draped Panel
Ranga, 03, Malabar.

Pages 120–123 Rod-Pocket Panels
Cotton gingham, yellow/white, John
Lewis.

Pages 126–131 Unlined Swedish Shade
Ziro, 27, Malabar.

Pages 132–137 Unlined Roman Shade
Cloche, Pink, Elanbach. Pole: Copes and
Timmins.

Pages 138–143 Lined Roman Shade
Jellabee, 02, Malabar. Variation: page 143,
Laura Ashley.

Pages 144–147 Relaxed Roman Shade
Antique French linen. Variation: page 147,
main fabric: Shanti, Rice, contrast fabric:
Shanti, Capsicum, Malabar.

Pages 148–153 Lined Swedish Shade

Main fabric: Patchwork Prairie; contrast fabric: Denim blue, Baer & Ingram. Variation: page153, main fabric: Dandelion Trellis cotton, Forget-me-not/ Cornflower; lining fabric: Stripe and Wiggle cotton, Sky blue/Denim, Vanessa Arbuthnott.

Pages 156–161 Soft Cornice

Trellis linen, Blue, Elanbach. Variations: page 160, Wilman; page 161, Kate Forman.

Pages 162–165 Gathered Valance

Wallgarden, Elanbach. Variation: page 165, Pret A Vivre.

Pages 166–169 Zigzag Panel Valance

Gingi 13, Malabar.

Pages 170–173 Upholstered Cornice

Main fabric: Stripe and Wiggle cotton, Sky blue/Denim; lining fabric: Dandelion Trellis cotton, Forget-me-not/Cornflower, Vanessa Arbuthnott.

Pages 176–179 Fabric Tiebacks

Blue Roses, Kate Forman. Variation: page 179, Laura Ashley.

Pages180–183 Soft Sash Tieback

Main fabric: Rowan Stripe, 02; lining fabric: Shot Cotton, Lime; binding fabric: Shot Cotton, Jade, Rowan. Variation: page 183, Malabar;

Other sources

US

A.C. Moore
866-342-8802
www.acmoore.com

Laura Ashley
www.lauraashley-usa.com

Calico Corners
1-800-213-6366
www.calicocorners.com

Cath Kidston
+44 (0) 1480 431 415
www.cathkidston.com

Coats and Clark
(800) 648-1479
www.coatsandclark.com

Cowtan & Tout
Distributors of Jane Churchill, Manuel Canovas and Colefax & Fowler
(212) 647-6900
www.cowtan.com

Craft Site Directory
Useful online resource
www.craftsitedirectory.com

Crafts etc.
1-800-888-0321
www.craftsetc.com

Emma One Sock
215-542-1082
www.emmaonesock.com

Hancock Fabrics
877-322-7427
www.hancockfabrics.com

Hobby Lobby
Stores throughout the US
www.hobbylobby.com

Husqvarna Viking
800-358-0001
www.husqvarnaviking.com

Jo-ann Fabric & Crafts
1-888-739-4120
www.joann.com

Michaels
1-800-642-4235
www.michaels.com

Rowan USA
+44 (0)1484 681881
www.knitrowan.com

Canada

B.B. Bargoons
1-800-665-9227
www.bbbargoons.com

Fabricland/Fabricville
Over 170 stores in Canada
www.fabricland.com
www.fabricville.com

InVU Drapery
905-828-2022
www.invudraperyco.com

Timmel Fabrics
1-877-825-9048
www.timmelfabrics.com

Wazoodle
1-866-473-4628
www.wazoodle.com

Photographic Credits

page 12, Biggie Best; page 13 left, Biggie Best, right, Biggie Best; page 14, Laura Ashley; page 15, Laura Ashley; page 16, top left, Wilman, top right, Biggie Best, below, Biggie Best; page 17, below left, Simon Whitmore; page 18, left, right, Biggie Best; page 19, left, right, Biggie Best.

Index

Entries in bold indicate photographs

BOSTON PUBLIC LIBRARY

3 9999 06251 273 4

Authors' Acknowledgments

Many thanks to all the people who helped us to make this book possible—we couldn't have done it without you!

Thanks to photographer extraordinaire, Mark Scott, who worked miracles to give us such light and airy pictures; Alicia Clarke and Rachel Whiting, who shot their way cheerfully through hundreds of step-by-steps; Gaye Hawkins, who made all the steps for us and who worked so hard to get them ready in time for the shoots; Jane Bolsover, who transformed our raw copy into clear, easy-to-understand instructions; editor Gillian Haslam, who smoothed the way and kept us all calm when the heat was on; publisher Cindy Richards, without whose encouragement the book wouldn't have seen the light of day; and our assistant Lily Hutton, who kept us all going with endless cups of tea.

Special thanks, too, to everyone who let us photograph their beautiful houses with not a word of complaint when we created complete chaos:
Eva Johnson, Joanna White, Vanessa Arbuthnott, Kate Forman, Christine Smith, Anne Bannell, Lizzie Hutton, Carol Gregory, Lisa Kirkham, and all the staff at Llangoed Hall, who looked after us so royally when we stayed there.

Many thanks to everyone who lent or gave us fabrics, products, and images to use for the projects, variations, and step-by-steps:
Emma Birch at Malabar, Vanessa Arbuthnott, Kate Forman, Rowan, Cabbages and Roses, Baer and Ingram, Jane Churchill, Ian Mankin, Cath Kidston, Laura Ashley, Biggie Best, Wilman, Rufflette, Walcot House, Husqvarna Viking for supplying us with the wonderful Quilt Designer sewing machine, Copes and Timmins, Swish, V.V. Rouleaux, Pret A Vivre, Ells & Farrier, and Coats Crafts UK.

Metric Conversion

¼ inch	6mm
½ inch	12mm
¾ inch	1.75cm
1 inch	2.5cm
2 inches	5cm
3 inches	7.5cm
4 inches	10cm
6 inches	15cm
9 inches	23cm
12 inches	30cm